TOM SHIELDS TOO

D0318852

Tom Shields *Too*

MORE TOM SHIELDS' DIARY

MAINSTREAM
PUBLISHING

EDINBURGH AND LONDON

Copyright © Tom Shields, 1993

All rights reserved

The moral right of the author has been asserted

First published in Great Britain in 1993 by
MAINSTREAM PUBLISHING COMPANY (EDINBURGH) LTD
7 Albany Street
Edinburgh EH1 3UG

ISBN 1 85158 504 4

No part of this book may be reproduced or transmitted in any form or by any
means without permission in writing from the publisher, except by a reviewer
who wishes to quote brief passages in connection with a review written for
insertion in a magazine, newspaper or broadcast

A catalogue record for this book is available from the British Library

Typeset in Plantin by Servis Filmsetting Ltd, Manchester

Printed in Great Britain by Butler and Tanner Ltd, Frome

CONTENTS

CONTENTS

POLITICS

A FEATURE of the intense security at all Tory party conferences is the team of policemen who have to check every drain and sewer in the vicinity and seal off the manhole covers. At a conference in Aberdeen, the cop whose task it was to spray yellow paint on the manholes, indicating that they had been checked, became exceedingly bored. As he waited to mark yet another drain, he spotted a dead cat. As a joke on his colleagues, he went ahead and added a set of yellow stripes to the corpse of the unfortunate deceased black pussy. Merry jape all round. But with so many manhole covers to paint, he forgot to go back and remove the feline cadaver from the public gaze. Thus it was that the local police station received a telephone call from a distressed elderly lady who had been out walking her dog when she discovered what she described as evidence of satanic rituals in the vicinity of the Aberdeen conference centre. The cop involved inevitably became known as Garfield.

JIMMY Allison, the Scottish Organiser of the Labour Party who retired early after less than gracious treatment at the hands of the party organisation, keeps active in the party and was canvassing in a Monklands council by-election. While the Labour activists were chapping doors, one householder said: 'I'm not voting Labour after what they did to Jimmy Allison.' The canvasser attempted to retrieve the situation by pointing out that Jimmy was still doing his bit for Labour just a couple of streets away. The potential voter thought for a moment and replied: 'Well, he must be daft then. I'm still not voting Labour.'

LORD James Douglas-Hamilton, the Edinburgh West Tory MP, is dreadfully nice and all the better for being a wee bit eccentric. It obviously runs in the family. Lord James, in his capacity as Scottish Home Affairs minister, received a letter from Haddington bemoaning the break-down of law and order in those parts. The letter went into some detail on vandalism, hooliganism and other patterns of behaviour not normally associated with that peaceful burgh. The letter received the minister's utmost and rapid attention. And so it should have. The letter was signed simply 'Mummy'.

LORD Fraser, even though he was then the Lord Advocate, had to go through the annual conference security rigmarole. Realising, somewhat late, that he would have to submit two passport photographs, he rushed to his local post office in Edinburgh. He inserted his £1.50 in the machine, pressed the button, and confidently awaited his four passport-sized pics. Out from the machine popped a postcard-size photograph of Edinburgh Castle with his physog inset in a corner. Examination of the machine showed that he had pressed the wrong button. But it could have been worse. Another option was to have his face on a tourist souvenir photograph of the Loch Ness monster.

THE Green Party candidate in the Kincardine by-election had to abandon his principles by borrowing a car for the duration of the campaign. This despite his philosophy that 'The only green car is a car that is left at home when you can get a bus.' Mr Campbell could have got a bus from his home in Ballater to the daily press conference in Stonehaven, but the bus leaves at 7.00 a.m. and takes forever. Mr Campbell, faced with the choice of spending all day on buses trying to get round the sprawling constituency, accepted the use of a car from his in-laws. It used unleaded petrol, of course.

GLASGOW Garscadden Labour MP Donald Dewar once came top of a poll of most romantic MPs conducted by House of Commons secretaries. Donald, who often comes across as a deeply serious man, was described by the secretaries as a Heathcliffe-type figure. But Mr Dewar did not live up to this romantic reputation when, during a meeting of the Scottish Constitutional Convention's executive, it was decided that the next meeting would be held on St Valentine's Day and he asked, 'When's that?'

JOHN Corrie, the Conservative candidate for Argyll at the 1992 General Election, had a wee gem of a campaign leaflet. It began: 'John Corrie was Member of Parliament for North Cunninghame until boundary changes altered the seat.' In other words he lost it to Labour. It went on: 'In 1979 he was awarded the Wilberforce Plague for humane work.' Actually, it was a plaque. Finally the leaflet gave a persuasive reason why Mr Corrie was the man for this rural seat: 'He was Scottish Shearing Champion in 1959, shearing 221 sheep in nine hours.'

THE *Shetland Times* in their excellent coverage of local boy Norman Lamont's first Budget, reported that his maternal grandfather, Charles Hughson, lived in a croft called Loot.

MICHAEL Hirst, who tried in 1992 to regain Bearsden and Milngavie for the Tories, paid a campaign visit to a geriatric unit at Canniesburn Hospital. It was not a great vote-catcher. As he left, one old dear was heard to ask: 'Who was that nice young doctor?'

THE late Gregor MacKenzie, Labour MP for Rutherglen, is remembered by his colleagues for his dry sense of humour. In his capacity as a Minister of State at the Department of Industry, Gregor was happily fielding questions in the House of Commons. One MP's query was disposed of with the usual Civil Service excuse: 'These statistics are not available . . . blah, blah . . . could only be gathered at disproportionate cost to the taxpayer . . .' Another MP stood up and asked: 'Why, then, are these statistics to be found in the current edition of the *Department of Industry Journal*?' 'That's a very good question,' said Mr MacKenzie. 'But not as good as the question I'll be asking when I get back to the Department of Industry.'

ONE of Lord James Douglas-Hamilton's ministerial tasks was to declare open the Dundee Advice Centre for Education and Training, a new joint effort between Scottish Enterprise Tayside and Dundee College of Further Education. As the Scottish Office announced at the time: 'The Minister will be presented with an honorary Scotvec module in public speaking.' Stick that in your CV, Jimmy.

FULL marks to the English politician who wanted to send a message to

David Blunkett, the Sheffield Labour MP. Taking full cognisance of Mr Blunkett's impaired sight, the man had the letter specially typed in braille . . . and then sent by fax.

SIR David Steel's memoirs, in which he recounted his adventures in Russia as a student, provoked from another source a tale about the trip which hadn't made it into the book. The Boy David was to address the hosts on behalf of the Scottish students at a dinner on the final evening. He spoke no Russian but decided to make an effort. He scribbled down two words he had seen on lavatory doors which would enable him to begin his speech with the Russian for 'Ladies and gentlemen . . .' This he did and received tumultuous applause. Later that evening he was to learn that the English translation for his words was 'toilets and urinals'.

A NATION ONCE AGAIN

A SCOT on holiday in Winchester was severely molested by mysterious insects in the hotel garden. When he went into dinner he asked the waitress if they had midges there. 'I'm sorry we don't,' she replied, 'but I'll send out for some.'

WE have become used to chronicling in the Diary the amazing ignorance (and we don't mean that in a bad way, by the way) of your average English person about Scotland and the Scottish way of life. We did not expect Labour's deputy leader Roy Hattersley to add to the great ledger of English idiocy. But he has. Mr Hattersley was interviewed in *Citizens*, the magazine of Charter 88, the organisation which is campaigning for a written constitution for the United Kingdom. The wide-ranging article touched on the question of devolution of power.

Mr H. had this to say: 'I propose that we create regions which do have real powers. There could be, for example, a different educational system in Scotland. But these powers will be granted to them by Parliament. It can't possibly be a

secession with Scotland announcing that they're taking all these powers.

Westminster has to give those powers to Scotland.' And, perhaps, when Westminster is giving Scotland its own educational system, they could throw in a separate Scottish legal system. With London's permission we could even have our own national rugby and football teams. The possibilities are endless. But we suppose, Mr Hattersley, that a separate Scottish Labour Party is out of the question.

THE obituary in the *Daily Telegraph* of Lt-Col. Richard Broad told of his derring-do when his regiment was surrounded by tanks at St Valery in France in June 1940. Lt-Col. Broad and some of his chaps made a break for it. The obituary told how 'the Englishmen, having chanced upon a timber yard, built a raft' to cross the River Seine. And how 'the Englishmen' were indebted to a French lady who helped them escape. And to which regiment did these Englishmen belong? None other than the Seaforth Highlanders. We suspect there might have been the odd Inverness man involved.

THE classified advertisement section of *The Highlander*, a magazine for exiled Scots, makes interesting reading. Recently advertised were these items for sale: 'Bagpipes, practice chanters, spats, kilts, glengarries, balmorals, hand-embroidered badges, sashes, bugles, drummers' aprons, Scottish/Irish and Masonic jewellery such as belt buckles and cap badges.'

Hardly surprising, you might think, until you reach the name and address of the firm offering these Celtic goods for sale – Merchandisers International of Maharajah Road, Sialkot, Pakistan.

SCOTS are fairly put in their place in Gibraltar. The customs form to be filled in at this last redoubt of empire includes the phrase: 'In the place where it says nationality, do not write "Scotland" or "Scottish". Scotland is not a nation. Scotland is only a province of England.'

THE *Dictionary of Russian Language*, written by a chap called S.I. Ozhegob, lists the word viski. This is better known to us as whisky, although the Russian pronunciation sounds uncommonly like how our national drink might be uttered late on of an evening. The Russians, typical of their disregard for small nation states, go on to define viski as 'strong English vodka'.

THE *Financial Times*, in its review of a play, *The Bruce*, at the Edinburgh Festival, sent us Scots homeward to rethink the situation, as the Corries so neatly put it in their song. The *FT* critic stated that the Scots lost the battle of Bannockburn. He went on to state that they proceeded, nevertheless, to issue the Declaration of Arbroath, asserting their desire to be free from foreign domination. 'All of this is broadly historically true,' said the man from the *Financial Times*. Or not, as the case may be. Perhaps he was confused by Flodden, Culloden, or Wembley in 1961.

AS Ithers See Us: *Business Life*, a magazine produced by British Airways, had an article about the psychology and cultural implications of choosing colours. Bill Dunning, managing director of Scantest, 'Europe's leading colour research specialists', was quoted as saying that when it comes to choosing carpets there is a 'distinct North–South colour divide in the United Kingdom. In the south they prefer soft pastel colours while in the north, particularly the north-east and Scotland, they favour richer colours.' The article continues: 'Bill Dunning happily admits that he has no idea why this should be, though one wag has suggested that the popularity of red carpets in Glasgow is based on practical considerations – hiding the bloodstains.' Stitch that, Jimmy, as we used to say in culture city.

A TASTE of Scotland: The menu for the Hong Kong Hilton's Scottish food fortnight included that well-known Caledonian delicacy 'A Quaich of Fried Haggis Balls'.

NOT content with stealing our whisky, our oil, and our ancient game of rugby, the English are now stealing our mountains. Droitwich Spa Round Table No. 605 are the baddies in this connection. They went on a sponsored mountain climb and, according to their report in the *Tablet*, the mag-azine of the Round Table of Britain and Ireland: 'We undertook the 32-mile trek across Snowdonia to raise money for charity . . . and found ourselves having to cross all 15 Munros on the way. A Munro is a British mountain peak over 3,000ft.' Haud on a minute. We thought the Munros were exclusively Scottish. Our colleagues on that great magazine *The Great Outdoors* confirmed that this is indeed so. Of the 296 peaks over 3,000ft in Britain, only the 277 located in Scotland can be called Munros, after Sir Shuggie of that ilk who first documented them. The 15 peaks in Wales are called, rather prosaically, 3,000-footers. If they're looking for a generic they could always start with Kinnocks, work their way through Secombes, Burtons, Dylans, or even Max-Boyces. England is graced with only four 3,000-footers. It is hardly worth the bother of giving them a name.

AN advert for a shortbread mould read: 'Our eight-inch shortbread mould is expertly hand-carved in Scotland with a pineapple motif – the traditional symbol of welcome and friendship.' The pineapple motif, on close inspection, looks awfy like a thistle.

THE Donkeys, a book which tells the story of the British Expeditionary Force in 1915, has been reissued in paperback. Some of the captions to the photographs will give pause to any veterans of the Battle of Loos in

September of that year – or indeed to descendants of those who lost their lives. One caption refers to 'looking back at the English parapet'. The parapet in question had been manned by the 2nd Cameronians. Another photograph is described as an English outpost and yet another as 'the English line'. The positions in question were held entirely by Highland regiments. *The Donkeys* was written by Tory MP Alan Clark who, until he retired at the election, was a Minister of State at the Ministry of Defence.

WHEN nationalist fervour was rife before the 1992 election there was a short debate on what you would call an independent Scottish currency. One suggestion was the mickle, with 1314 mickles making a muckle. The muckle would float or sink with the punt. A jibe at a well-known politician who transferred allegiances from Labour to SNP was that 'we'll need a 30 pieces o' sillar note' for the new currency. There was strong support for a national name as the French do with the franc. Ours could be the jock. A jock would consist of a 100 weans. And 10 jocks would be a tamson, made up of 1,000 of his weans.

A LETTER from the Next Directory to a resident of Benbecula, who wished to do some business with the mail-order firm, said: 'Unfortunately we are unable to send you a copy of

the directory as we cannot send goods abroad and deal in foreign currencies. The reason for this is firstly the high cost of postage and secondly that we have no facilities for customs procedures for exporting.' Next suggested that if the Benbeculan still wanted goods from their directory, he ask a friend or relative with an address in the UK to act as an intermediary.

GAZETTEER

THEY behave in strange ways in Motherwell if the evidence in the following court case is any guide: a barman was cleared of starting a fire at his uncle's pub. We quote this snippet of evidence from the *Motherwell Times*'s coverage of the trial: 'He [the accused] blamed one of the pub customers with whom he had indulged in a drunken bout of Sumo wrestling in the pub a few hours before the fire was discovered. The court heard that a police officer called to the fire found the accused with a tartan rug over his head hiding behind a Christmas tree in a close near the pub.'

ALSO from Motherwell is the tale of an industrial tribunal where a chap claimed unfair dismissal. His firm pointed out that he had thrown a cup of tea over a female colleague who was his former girlfriend. He claimed provocation because she had been nagging him in sign language. The tribunal found him two-thirds to blame.

IT was inevitable that a joke should emerge linking the Bank of Credit and Commerce International and the globetrotting Motherwell District Council. Apparently, initial fears that the Motherwell council might have lost some funds lodged with BCCI proved groundless since the Motherwell council keeps all its cash in travellers' cheques.

FROM Cunninghame District Council we heard the story of a councillor who had been deputed to go to London to accept an award from the British Tourist Authority. The gong was to be handed out by a royal personage at a lavish ceremony in a hotel in the Strand. The tribune of the people was duly given his air tickets, hotel voucher, and invitation. Reading the words '7pm for 7.15pm' on this last document, the councillor asked a council official: 'Are you sure we should be going to this? It seems an awful expense just for 15 minutes.'

MEANWHILE, back in the real world of local government politics, members of the SNP opposition group on Cumbernauld and Kilsyth District Council put down a motion of 'no confidence' in Labour Provost Rosemary McKenna for her chairmanship of the council. One of the grounds cited in the motion is that she

'repeatedly refuses to accept motions of no confidence'.

DUMFRIES and Galloway Regional Council Public Library Byelaws ensure that users obey a strict code of conduct:

- No person shall spit in the library.
- No person shall sleep in the library after having been requested to refrain from doing so by the librarian.
- Any person who in the opinion of the librarian is intoxicated or disorderly or so unclean in his person as would be likely to cause offence to other users of the library, shall not enter or use the library.
- No person shall lie on the furniture or fittings of the library or on the floor thereof except with the consent of the librarian.
- No person who is suffering from a contagious or infectious disease shall enter or use the library.

GORDON Murray, a former provost of Cumbernauld, lodged a housing application that could best be described as unusual. In a letter to Cumbernauld and Kilsyth District Council's chief executive, Mr Murray listed a number of circumstances which, he says, made a priority of the application by him and his wife, fellow councillor Margaret Murray. He said that the 'medical conditions which prompt this request' included:

- 'I have only one eye and my eyesight in the remaining eye is failing.'
- 'I have numerous gunshot wounds.'
- 'Most Labour councillors and some officials of the district council are convinced I have been suffering from Alzheimer's disease for some time. (Unfortunately my numerous medical consultants have not been able to confirm this to date, otherwise I might have escaped liability for poll tax.)'
- 'My once active sex life has become a distant memory.'
- 'My fair skin makes me liable to a number of skin diseases ranging from skin cancer to chronic dandruff (a dandruff so severe it will not react to Head & Shoulders or any of the modern miracle cures!)'
- 'My various medical conditions are aggravated by the fact that I am a compulsive eater and suffer from gross obesity.'

The other medical points ranged from arthritis of the spine, a disease of the blood vessels, and a heart attack.

While this was a touching letter, council officials were puzzled as to why it had been written, since the councillors Murray already had a perfectly good house in Cumbernauld. It appeared that the letter was an attempt at satire, commenting on the fact that a Labour councillor had recently been granted a house on health grounds.

IT is no easy task to foil the talented thieves of the Glasgow garden suburb of Drumchapel. One anecdote concerned the construction of a garage to house a local school minibus. On the assumption that what ain't fastened down will be lifted, the authorities, on delivering the bricks with which to build the garage, thoughtfully provided also a watchman, a watchman's hut, and an Alsatian dog. One evening the watchman sloped off for a quick pint. On his return, he discovered that the bricks had indeed remained secure. However, both the watchman's hut and the Alsatian had been stolen.

ON a rare foray to the Borders we were asked: 'What label does a Hawick girl have on her knickers?' To which we replied: 'We don't know. What label does a Hawick girl wear on her knickers?' Answer: 'Next.'

A TALE from Ayrshire which sounds too silly to be true but we are assured is not apocryphal. It happened in Dalry which might explain a lot. The scene is the Roche chemical plant in this douce Ayrshire toon. A Swiss engineer was on secondment from the parent company. His English was no' richt guid, to let you understaun'. One of the locals decided that what the Swiss chap needed was a book to help him with his English. The Swiss chap was delighted with this kind offer and duly read the book with the efficiency and thoroughness for which his nation are famous. He came in the next day with a few supplementary questions for the Dalry man. 'What means "Michty Me!" and "Whit's wrang wi' the Bairn?"' Yes, he had been given a Broons book to study.

LAW

THE Airdrie criminal element remember fondly Elish McPhilomy despite her attempts as a depute procurator-fiscal to lock them away. Indeed at the get-together to mark Ms McPhilomy's departure to work in Edinburgh, a well-known local offender turned up clutching an impressive bouquet of flowers. These he handed over while delivering a short speech to the effect that even though the lovely Ms McPhilomy had personally been responsible for an adverse result on each of his last six appearances, he was full of admiration for her. At this point the well-mannered recidivist departed, spoiling the effect of his gesture more than somewhat with his parting shot: 'By the way, I stole the flowers.'

THE late Bellamy Cay, who was perhaps the most senior junior of the faculty of advocates, specialised in divorce actions in those halcyon days when such cases were still heard in the Court of Session. He augmented his earnings from renting out bits of property. He was engaged one day in the Court of Session in trying to disengage his female client from her husband on the grounds of unreasonable behaviour. It appears that he had not had much time to interview his client but was sure that she would be able to provide enough ammunition to win the case. Just tell us in your words about your husband's behaviour, he asked the client. She explained that he was particulaly messy around the house. He would burn carpets, stub cigarette ends out on the parquet flooring, and generally have no respect for furniture and fittings. 'This is outrageous behaviour!' Mr Cay exclaimed. His lordship said that he had heard much worse. The woman, urged by Mr Cay for more detail, explained embarrassedly that her husband would occasionally, under the influence of excess alcohol, urinate in the hall cupboard instead of in the toilet. This totally unacceptable behaviour roused Mr Cay to near fury. Again his lordship agreed that it was a pretty poor show but hardly amounted to gross cruelty. 'But, your lordship,' explained Mr Cay, 'they live in one of my flats.'

FROM Dumbarton, that unruly legal province on the north-west of the Clyde, such was the volume of work caused by people up to nae good that an annexe had to be opened, consisting of two new courts. The annexe was located through the wall from a public house. Thus justice was dispensed daily in the court to the distant but audible accompaniment of honky-tonk music from next door. In these circumstances, Sheriff John Fitzsimmons was doing his best to maintain the dignity of his court. One accused was found guilty. Sheriff Fitzsimmons asked the defence lawyer to make his plea in mitigation. Just as he was about to do so, the court was treated to a rendition from next door of that old Connie Francis favourite *Who's Sorry Now?*

A POLISMAN giving evidence in an assault case at Glasgow Sheriff Court was asked to tell the court what had been said during the affray. He told how one of the accused had shouted to him: 'Away and sook your plums!' The fiscal, understandably, asked the polisman if he could elaborate on what this unusual imprecation might mean. At this point the defence lawyer (no less a person than Joe Beltrami) leapt to his feet with the words: 'Don't answer that. You're not an expert witness. You're not a greengrocer.'

A CHILDREN'S panel was discussing whether or not a child should be taken into care. The lawyer acting for the parents was trying to establish when a certain event occurred. Could they pin down the date by associating it to a birthday or some other notable event? After a moment's thought the wife turned to her beloved and asked: 'When wis it again that you stabbed me?'

A SOCIAL inquiry at Furryboots City Sheriff Court said of the offender: 'He does not seek to excuse himself of responsibility for the offences. In fact, he accepts responsibility for all charges, including those dropped by the procurator-fiscal.'

THE centenary dinner of the XIII Club, a select gathering of Glasgow intellectuals which has a get-together every 13 February, was regaled with a tale from the days when lawyers were gentlemen. Sorry, I'll rephrase that – when lawyers were even more gentlemanly than they are today. The speaker in question was Ron Neil, the man in charge of BBC Television news and current affairs. He was referring to his father, John Neil. Neil Senior was so proper in his behaviour that, when one day he was accosted by a footpad and relieved of his wallet and gold watch, he pursued the perpetrator shouting the words: 'Stop alleged thief! Stop alleged thief!'

A CASE at Edinburgh Sheriff Court resulted in a most unusual unanimous verdict of not proven. The verdict did not surprise one experienced legal practitioner who remarked: 'It always happens after that film has been on the telly.' That film, it transpires, is *Twelve Angry Men*, Sydney Lumet's gripping tale of how one man of principle convinces the rest of a jury to acquit a man accused of murder on grounds of reasonable doubt. The film had, indeed, been on BBC2 the previous Sunday night.

TWO young criminal types in Ayr swiped a bag containing half a hundredweight of 10p coins from a shop in the Honest Toon. They then made their way to an amusement arcade to spend their ill-gotten gains on the various machines. The extent of their loot excited the suspicion of the manager who dialled 999. The two master criminals spotted the arriving polis and made good their escape. The boys in blue were about to give chase when their attention was drawn to the sound of the photo booth churning out four pin-sharp, self-incriminating pictures of the villains.

THERE was a case in Glasgow involving murder and mayhem, the full details of which need not concern youse gentle readers. A great deal of the evidence had to do with the fact that various miscreants were under the effects of drink and a drug called Temazepam. One middle-aged lady member of the jury was heard to remark to a fellow juror: 'I think I understand it all so far. Except

for the bits about the tomato plants.'

ONE cannot accuse Joe Beltrami, the leading lawyer, of not doing his homework. Joe caused some head-scratching in Loretto's, a Glasgow Italian restaurant, when he challenged his lunchtime companions, a team of legal eaglets, to name the river which flows through Florence. 'The Tiber,' quoth one. 'No, no,' said Joe.

'How about the Po?' suggested another. 'Dear, dear,' said Joe (who always says everything twice), shaking his head. 'Everyone knows it is the Arno. The Arno. I'm shocked you don't know. Shocking, shocking.'

As the lunch ended, one of the company furtively approached the Italian restaurateur. 'Go and say to Joe how much you enjoyed as a boy in Florence walking beside the river Tiber,' he suggested. The Italian looked dismayed. 'I cannot,' he protested. 'But it's just for a wee joke,' said the lawyer. 'No,' said the Italian, 'it cannot be done.' 'Why not?' asked the lawyer. 'Because,' replied the harassed Italian, 'Big Joe, he ask me just a half-hour ago – hey, what ees the river that run through Florence?'

THE common-law widow, if there is such a thing, of one of the victims of a gangland slaying proved a formidable witness when the case came to the High Court. She was asked if her man was of regular habits. She snapped: 'His tea was oan the table at five. If he wisnae there he didn't get it.' Asked if

he had any other girlfriends, she smiled grimly. 'He had wan wance.' Pause. 'Why? Are ye gonnie surprise me?'

Another witness poured scorn on the evidence that the murder victim had another lady friend, Miss X. He said: 'He was a big, brave boy – but no way would he have been parked with Miss X outside his girlfriend's house. First, she would have beaten him up. Then she would have beaten up Miss X. Then she would have beaten up the car.'

In the same trial a witness, a hardened criminal, described a fellow villain as: 'Not a very nice person.' Asked for clarification he replied: 'He's a f****** toerag!'

A LEGAL eaglet exhibited a lack of knowledge of the ways of the lower orders when he was defending a citizen charged with recklessly discharging an air pistol. He decided that the only fruitful route for an acquittal was to claim that the air pistol was not a vandal's plaything but was used for hunting. 'What does the accused hunt with the gun?' was the not unreasonable question from the man on the bench. The lawyer consulted his client who could only say that it was a slug gun. 'My client uses the gun to hunt slugs, your honour . . .' he told an astonished court.

A YOUNG lawyer was appearing at Ayr Sheriff Court for a client who had an appalling record for offences of dishonesty and was about to be sentenced for another. In his attempt to mitigate his client's behaviour the lawyer told the sheriff that virtually all of the accused's previous convictions were drink-related. His client, he went on, had decided to turn over a new leaf and had been attending a local rehabilitation unit. His treatment had been going very well, he told the sheriff, who seemed suitably impressed. Then the lawyer added: 'I would be misleading your lordship if I didn't tell you that there have been one or two hiccups along the way.'

A LAWYER acting for a man on a charge of rape received a visit from the accused's wife. The lawyer had the difficult task of explaining to her that things were not looking too good. He explained that the evidence was pretty strong and her man was facing a substantial jail sentence. 'I know,' she said, 'and, of course, he's done it before.' The puzzled lawyer consulted his files and said: 'Are you sure? I don't see any record here of a previous conviction for rape.' 'Oh, aye,' she says. 'He raped the wumman up the stair.' 'Did the case go to court?' the lawyer asked. 'Oh, no. She didnae tell the polis,' the woman explained. 'We've got awfy good neighbours.'

BAILIE Bill Aitken was doing his regular stint on the bench at Glasgow District Court. In the dock was a prostitute whom he fined £100, the going rate. As usual he granted time to pay at £10 per week. Normally these ladies of the night pay up without complaint. But on this occasion the bailie noticed a frisson of concern from the accused. 'I can't afford £10 a week,' she complained. 'Why not?' enquired the bailie. 'I've hurt my back,' she explained. For once, the bailie, noted for his tough sentencing, was moved to mercy. He granted time to pay at £3 a week.

CHINA Syndrome: A woman was giving evidence against her husband who was accused of beating her up. The defence lawyer, struggling for a line, asked if it was not the case that her husband had suffered a serious head injury and had a metal plate in his skull. 'Aye,' she said, 'but there are times when I think he's got a cup and saucer in there as well.'

FROM Stornoway Sheriff Court we heard the story of a young man who pled guilty to stealing a quantity of frozen prawns, some of which, he admitted, he had sold later at the back door of a local hotel. Sheriff Donald Booker Milburn, who had flown over from Inverness the day before to take the court, duly fined the accused.

Then, recalling that he had stayed at this very hotel and further recalling his dinner menu, he reflected that his connection with the case was closer than merely passing sentence: 'I think I may have eaten some of the evidence in this case.'

BARLINNIE

BARLINNIE is an open prison. The thousand or so inmates who are dubbed up in their peters as you read this may disagree, but what we are talking about is access from interested external parties to the great micro-cosm of prison life that is the Bar-L. From governor Peter Withers down, the staff proudly boast that there is no hidden agenda at Barlinnie.

When a well-known Scottish tabloid newspaper asked the Bar-L authorities to comment on allegations of prisoner maltreatment, the reporter was invited to visit any part of the prison and ask any questions. The reporter did so and, as deputy gover-nor Robbie Glenn says, 'gave us a clean bill of health'.

'So, what will you be writing about us, then?' Robbie Glenn asked the journalist. 'Nothing. There's no story here,' was the reply. The story of Barlinnie's new regime since the rooftop riots has been well document-ed. The visitor's trail is well worn. Just before my visit, photographers from the Cranhill Arts Project were in the prison at seven thirty a.m. one Sunday morning to capture the slop-ping-out parade for their archive of Glasgow life.

You would be as likely to meet a party from a woman's guild as a seri-ous investigative reporter as the Bar-L pursues its open-door policy; open doors for visitors that is.

My invitation to visit Barlinnie came after I wrote a wee story in the *Herald* Diary about a shop in Glasgow which was selling a novelty whisky called Barlinnie Bevvy, without per-mission from the authorities. I wrote that we hoped it appealed to the gov-ernor's sense of humour. Peter Withers was quickly on the phone with the question: 'What sense of humour?' He then said it was all in good fun and suggested that a bottle of the whisky be delivered to the prison, presumably for their archives.

Then deputy governor Robbie Glenn picked up on the Diary's refer-ence to Barlinnie as 'Riddrie's best-known B&B'. 'We prefer to think of it as the Riddrie Hilton,' I heard him regale an audience during one of his famous after-dinner speeches. 'It is possibly Glasgow's most successful hotel. It has high room-occupancy rates. Unlike other hotels, our resi-dents are carefully vetted and always arrive with a police escort. They are obviously happy with the service.

They return with astonishing regularity, sometimes bringing friends and family with them.'

Robbie Glenn invited me to sample a taste of Barlinnie with the words: 'You'll find it very interesting and once you leave you won't want to come back as an uninvited guest.'

The Victorian bleakness of Barlinnie brings to mind prisoner Wilde's words written about his spell in Reading Gaol:

The vilest deeds like poison weeds,
Bloom well in prison air;
It is only what is good in Man
That wastes and withers there:
Pale Anguish keeps the heavy gate,
And the warder is despair.

In my case the warder was John McRoberts, who, I suspect, was given the job as my tour guide because he is a leading exponent of the Bar-L sense of humour. (He is not a warder by the way; they are officers, senior officers, principal officers, and governors.) He is a veteran of the riots at both Barlinnie and Shotts who sometimes daydreams about a post at an open prison in the countryside where the most pressing problem can be whose turn it is to milk the cows. But he knows he would get bored and miss the day-to-day challenge of man-management and crisis control. Or keeping the prisoners off the roof as it is also known.

John McRoberts is the Care Bear in E Hall. The official job description is caseworker and his task is to look after the prisoners' welfare and speed them as humanely and efficiently as possible through their prison careers. He is no soft touch, but has a genuine concern for his charges. A concern which he can express either in sociological language (for which he takes some stick from certain of his fellow officers) or in very straightforward terms.

'Most of the people I have to deal with in here are social inadequates with chronic alcohol-abuse problems which have placed them outside society,' he says. Or, to put it another way: 'Most of the people locked up in Barlinnie wouldn't hurt a fly. Then they go outside and get stuck into that singing ginger and get done for breach of the peace.

'Look at old Bob,' he says, referring to a long-term Barlinnie resident whose speciality is breach with a spot of shoplifting. 'He goes out vowing never to return. Then he has a few drinks, needs money for a few more, pops into Marks & Spencer, and thinks he's invisible. You're the worst shoplifter in Glasgow, aren't you, Bob?'

In his Care Bear's den in E Hall, John McRoberts keeps a big tank of tropical fish. When a prisoner comes in to discuss a problem, he is always sat in front of the fish tank. Often there is little John can do about the prisoner's problem. Usually they just want a bit of attention, a change of routine, and a therapeutic look at the fish.

'Did you phone the kennels, Mr

McRoberts?' a prisoner asks. His alsatian is doing time in kennels while he is in the Bar-L. The Care Bear has to keep in touch with the kennels to give progress reports on the well-being of the dog. It is hardly I-Was-a-Prisoner-on-the-Chain-Gang stuff.

Another prisoner has a more unusual family problem. He is wondering how his father is getting on. His father has left the relative safety of darkest Ayrshire to be a mercenary in Croatia.

So what makes a good prison officer? A brains trust of officers with varying lengths of service consider this topic over a coffee in the office of C Hall, a melting pot where upwards of 250 untried prisoners of all persuasions are contained. You need to be a psychologist, a psychiatrist, a kindly social worker, a strict disciplinarian, a keen student of the criminal mind . . . 'And it helps if you're good at the boxing. Just ask Andy,' interjects an officer. Andy Ritchie has been attacked twice in recent months. He says: 'This job is full of surprises. One morning you open a cell door to a reasonably polite greeting, the next to a punch in the nose.' Andy Ritchie says he still has a 'reasonable relationship' with both the attackers.

He grew up in Blackhill, the tough housing estate near Barlinnie. While it is common for the career path of your average Blackhill youth to take him to the Bar-L, it is unusual for him to end up as a custodian. 'You could say it was not a great culture shock for me

to come to work in Barlinnie,' Andy Ritchie says.

Like every other young officer, Andy Ritchie had to learn fast. 'You have your basic training but nothing can prepare you for the real thing.' From your first day, when some lag will look at the newcomer's new uniform and opine: 'Your ma's turned ye oot nice,' the tyro officer is on a steep and interesting learning curve.

To the wall of the office in C Hall, there is affixed a notice bearing a piece of Bar-L cracker-barrel philosophy aimed at the younger members of staff: 'Old age and treachery will always overcome youth and skill.'

By necessity, Barlinnie humour is a black humour. All human life is there and most of the prejudices. There is a true story about the unfortunate who found himself inside for having sex with a dog. For his first meal, a bone was thrown into the cell. He asked what was going on to be told that if it was good enough for his girlfriend, it was good enough for him. This was many years ago and would, of course, never happen in these more enlightened days.

Also from darker days there is the story of a huge African who found himself incarcerated in Barlinnie. The warders promised him a special meal as a change from the routine. At teatime they threw the smallest on-duty warder into his cell.

These days the humour is gentler but still with an edge. A mischievous officer asked for volunteers for a party to go and wash the windows at Cornton Vale. The prospect of a trip out-side, not to mention the chance of some female company, meant that in no time at all the squad was assembled and ready to march off, buckets and cloths in hand. It was then they realised, amid the gales of laughter from officers and fellow prisoners, how unlikely a mission they had volunteered for.

Then there was the prisoner from England who had to come to Glasgow to give evidence at a trial. He left his open prison on his own, travelled by train to Glasgow, took a bus to Barlinnie, and knocked on the door to announce that he had arrived for his night's bed and breakfast. Rules is rules and he was taken in, handcuffed and locked in a holding cell until they could work out where to put him.

There is, of course, much scope for the practical joke. Like the one played on a senior officer who had a mania for cleanliness, an almost impossible pursuit in a prison more than 100 years old. 'What's that?' he would bark. 'Dust, sir!' or, 'Litter, sir!' would be the reply to an obvious question.

A piece of newspaper was covered in brown sauce and left out for inspection. 'What's that?' came the almost apoplectic inquiry. The prisoner in the cell stuck his finger in the mess, licked it, and replied casually: 'Shite, sir!'

Inmates like Coutsie are a rich source of grim humour. Even when he's outside the Bar-L, which isn't often, his life tends to get inextricably mixed with the prison. His problem in life is too much of the singing ginger. There he was standing at a corner in Duke Street, sipping at his can of strong lager, when he espied the Barlinnie bus taking its cargo back from the courts. The bus stopped at the traffic lights. Coutsie enquired of the driver, whom he knows well, if there was any chance of a pound for a drink. The driver declined. Coutsie lay down in front of the bus. The driver relented, gots down from the bus and gave Coutsie his £1 blackmail money.

Coutsie's job at the prison includes helping the chaplains set up for services. Given his position of trust, he says, he would never think of assuaging his thirst by swigging the communion wine. 'Anyway, it's only one per cent,' he says.

It's easy to laugh at Coutsie's patter and forget the man behind the well-lived-in face, the sort of face you get in Tam Shepherd's, suggests an officer. Or from a lifetime of cheap drink.

Coutsie did his first spell in Barlinnie in 1961. The longest he has been out since is five weeks. He has 205 convictions, mostly for breach of the peace. During banter with John McRoberts and other officers, Coutsie proclaims that he taught them everything they know. But he is sadly lacking skills which will sustain him out of a prison environment. Apart from a skill in hijacking prison buses, he is adept at rooting out caches of booze hidden in the environs of Celtic Park by fans anxious to avoid the penalties of the Criminal Justice Scotland Act without losing their carry-out. It is hardly a training for life.

While the Bar-L undoubtedly has its share of tough men, the majority of its population are like Coutsie, the flotsam and jetsam of society. People who should be receiving treatment and rehabilitation. The sad fact is that it is cheaper for the authorities to keep these people in prison and this is increasingly the case as hospitals close their doors on the problem.

Another significant part of the prison population are those in for car theft, driving while banned, or some other motoring offence. A whole generation of young men appear to be locked up because of their obsession with motor cars. At one point, after meeting six of these motor villains in succession, I wondered if there were any real violent men in the Bar-L. Then I met the man who had stabbed his girlfriend. But, as his pal said in mitigation, if you met her, you'd stab her too.

There are, of course, some of the real thugs who can make life a misery for their fellow inmates. Drugs are the big currency in prisons these days. The more successful the police are in putting drug dealers and users away, the bigger a problem it becomes for the prison service. Thus a new inmate, even someone not remotely connected with the drugs culture, can find himself involved. Called to the visiting-room, he might find himself confronted by a strange woman who

will give him a lingering kiss and pass a packet of drugs into his mouth. His task is to swallow it, bring it out (either up or down), and hand the contents over to the drugs barons. Or else.

Families might find there is a knock on the door and be handed a wee parcel which they have to smuggle in on their next visit. Or else. (To digress from the subject of drugs, older officers reminisce about the good old days when the lags would try to alleviate the boredom of Barlinnie life by making a batch of hooch with some raisins, sugar and yeast from the cookhouse. To avoid detection, the Barlinnie brew had to be drunk young, resulting in a laxative as well as an intoxicating effect. One cheeky bunch of hooch-makers kept the stuff in the fire bucket outside the senior officer's door.)

The new regime at Barlinnie, introduced after the roof riots, is aimed at controlling the hard men and making the individual prisoner less vulnerable. The dining-rooms system has been abandoned. With upwards of 200 men in one room, there were never enough officers on hand to prevent intimidation or react at a flashpoint. Prisoners now eat in their cells and are moved to work and recreation in smaller numbers. The officers feel more in control. The prisoners feel safer.

Robbie Glenn, with his enthusiasm for the place, claims there is probably more violence in your average Glasgow primary school playground than there is in Barlinnie. I thought I had stumbled across what the aforementioned tabloid journalist might have called a story. The windscreen of the yellow hired van used to transport food from the cookhouse to the halls was pitted with gunshot holes. A failed escape attempt? No, the van had been on hire recently to a well-known Scottish arts organisation for a tour of France. The driver had fallen foul of a French farmer who took a pot-shot at the windscreen.

If Barlinnie is a safer place these days for its uninvited guests, and the conditions are less crowded, the reality of incarceration is no less awful. The admission hall gives an immediate impression of abandon hope all ye

who enter here. In a setting of Victorian squalor, the new inmate is divested of his worldly trappings, showered, issued with a set of clean but well-worn prison clothes, given a Barlinnie bowl (his first taste of prison food), then locked in a four-foot square holding cell while awaiting allocation to a prison hall. It is a soul-destroying experience, even for the most hardened criminals.

On one of my visits, the sound from one of the holding cells was a young man sobbing and calling out for his mother. The same young man who was pictured smiling as he left court with a life sentence for murder. But his future, such as it is, will not be at Barlinnie. Apart from the Special Unit with its infamous inhabitants, the Bar-L caters for prisoners serving sentences up to 18 months. Their main concern will be to do their time, avoid trouble, land a good job in the gnome-painting shed, and get access to as many creature comforts as possible.

Which brings us to the Barlinnie food. The cooks are proud of what they achieve on a budget of £6.38 for a whole week's food for each prisoner. One of the governors has to sample the menu each day and write his comments in the book. Robbie Glenn likes his prison food and puts in comments such as: 'The liver *au poivre* is an interesting addition to the menu.'

The old standard fare of porridge, mince and stews has been replaced by curries, sweet and sour dishes, and when there is a bargain to be had at the fish market, salmon or trout. Me? I had the Barlinnie bridie. Homemade, like everything at the Bar-L, delicious and containing more meat than us chaps on the outside are used to.

The pink custard was something else. I didn't taste it. Its very appearance, I'm sure, is against the Geneva Convention.

J. IRVINE SMITH

THE occasion of Sheriff J. Irvine Smith's retirement caused a flurry of anecdote and memories. The sheriff, for long a terrorist and a humorist in the bailiwicks of Glasgow and Greenock, had semi-retired to Rothesay to be the only law west of Gourock.

A famous client of Irvine Smith's was the late Barney Noone. It is fair to say that he had developed a rapport with Sheriff J. This went as far as poetry. One day, having been found guilty, Mr Noone wrote a message in verse which he asked be passed to the Bench. The sheriff read the poetic plea in mitigation and, without hesitation, pronounced: 'Thirty days hath September, April, June, and Barney Noone.'

IRVINE Smith was dealing with the recalcitrants and recidivists of Dunoon, a bevy of chaps who had failed to meet their commitments in the matter of paying fines. The sheriff began by asking one defaulter if he smoked, or drank the demon alcohol. In moderation, the man replied. A couple of pints and 20 fags a day. That amounted to nearly £30 a week; so, the sheriff was sure, the arrears could be made up swiftly, like that very day.

It turned out that this was possible. It also transpired that, through the bush telegraph, not another defaulter that day turned out to be a smoker or a drinker. But Sheriff Smith's most withering comment of the day was reserved for the man who had promised but failed to pay his fine at £10 a week. What offer did he have for the court, Sheriff Smith asked. The man replied that he could manage £2 a fortnight. The sheriff dismissed this with the words: 'I'm here to dispense justice, not to run a catalogue.'

THE sheriff was famous for his short, sharp custodial method of dealing with chaps who had fallen behind with payment of their fines. In his first such court at Greenock, he was banging away defaulters to such a fine tune that the polisman in charge of the Bar-L bus felt it necessary to approach Irvine Smith in his chambers during a recess to inform him that the vehicle was already full and that there was no more room at the inn. The sheriff casually reached for a copy of the Yellow Pages and handed it to the cop with the words: 'I believe you'll find it under coach hire.'

IRVINE Smith was a hard man when it came to the question of bail. There is the story of the traumatic time when he suffered a heart attack in court. As he was helped into his chambers, he managed to whisper to a court official: 'Tell him bail's refused.'

THE sheriff's uncompromising attitude often elicited a response from the accused. As one chap was being led away for a taste of porridge, he let slip the phrase 'F****** bastard'. Irvine Smith, with his keen hearing, picked this up. Asked to elaborate, the felon claimed it was not a reference to the sheriff. Irvine Smith begged to differ: 'I don't see anyone else in the courtroom who answers that description.'

AFTER having heard a case Irvine Smith asked the accused: 'Have you anything to say?' 'F*** all,' replied the accused in muffled tones. 'What did he say?' Sheriff J. asked the clerk to the court. 'F*** all,' replied the clerk. 'Funny,' said the sheriff. 'I'm sure I saw his lips move.'

LEN Murray, the solicitor, recounts two Irvine Smith stories of a slightly perverse nature. Two homosexuals appeared before the sheriff, having pled guilty to the type of conduct which was then still regarded as criminal. He deferred sentence on them to give them the chance to 'pull themselves together'. The sheriff's penchant for original repartee is further illustrated in the story of a transvestite. He deferred sentence on him, telling him to 'go away and be a good girl'.

HAVING listened to an accused recite his version of events, Irvine Smith leaned forward and told him: 'You are a fecund liar.' 'Oh no I'm not,' said the accused. 'I'm telling the f****** truth!'

A WITNESS being examined in front of Irvine Smith was asked by the defence lawyer: 'What is your occupation?' 'Humphin' ginger at Springwells,' he replied. 'What?' said the sheriff. The lawyer explained: 'My client is endeavouring to inform the court that he is employed in a menial capacity by a well-known firm situated on the outskirts of Blantyre, which is engaged in the manufacture of aerated waters.' 'Well,' said Sheriff Irvine Smith. 'Why couldn't the fellow have said that in the first place?'

AN accused, prior to being sentenced by Sheriff Irvine Smith, declared: 'As God is my judge I am innocent!' Sheriff J. quickly replied: 'He's not. I am. You are fined £50.'

ADDRESSING a businessman's luncheon club, Irvine Smith intoned: 'Gentlemen. You see, standing before you, the Messiah.' A hush fell as the audience began to ponder the sanity of this pillar of the establishment. 'Yes, gentlemen, the Messiah,' he went on. 'Only this morning an unfortunate was dragged before me in court and I heard him mutter, "Oh, it's him, Jesus Christ".'

A CONVICTED wife-beater, having copped a stiffish nine months, protested that he had 'only hit her the wanst'. 'Oh well, then,' said the sheriff, 'you do not qualify for our quantity discount.'

A LAWYER friend was dining in the Malmaison with Irvine Smith. It was a cold day in the mid-1960s, when the mini-skirt was in vogue, and the legal eagles were transfixed by the entrance of two young women whose skirts would have qualified as wide belts had they been a fraction shorter. Regaining his breath and aplomb, the sheriff dryly remarked: 'If they're not careful they'll get chaps between their legs.'

IRVINE Smith was sentencing a bruiser in the dock to three months. 'Three months?' quoth he, in disdain. 'I could dae that staunin' on ma' heid.' 'In that case,' replied Sheriff Smith, 'you can have another three months for contempt of court. Perhaps that will help you find your feet.'

THE LIVELY ARTS

JOHN Taylor is an artist who thinks deeply. A quiet, intellectual man, as is testified by his works which you will find at the Glasgow Print Studio. But Mr Taylor is not a man of the world – as is testified by his tale of getting a haircut. The artist was persuaded to have his leonine mane attended to, for a change, not in a barber's shop but in a salon in the West End of Glasgow.

Suitably primed, Mr Taylor knew that he would have to don a back-to-front goonie and that he would have his hair washed by an assistant coiffeuse. Everything went well until he was summoned to have his locks shampooed. Instead of sitting down and leaning his head back, as us sophisticates know it is done, he knelt on the chair and stuck his head into the sink. Much to the amazement of the assistant coiffeuse who obviously had never heard how mammy used to wash the wean's hair at the jawbox.

THE Diary's dear colleague Andy Young has spent many years reporting on showbusiness and the livelier arts. Unaccountably, Andy has never put into print a wee incident during one of his many sojourns at the Edinburgh Festival. Andy's son was through at the Festival and, after taking in a few shows, met his dad for a spot of supper. Unfortunately, Young Jnr missed his last train and Andy offered to put him up in the spare single bed in his hotel room. Andy was trying to explain at length to the night porter about how his son had missed his train to Glasgow and would be staying overnight. The porter interrupted him with the words: 'It's all right, sir. You don't have to explain. This is the Edinburgh Festival after all.'

DEPT of being Dead Cultured: Mr Brian McMaster, the director of the Edinburgh Festival, received an unusual and touching farewell gift from his former colleagues at Welsh National Opera. It was a swearbox in the shape of a WC. The gift apparently reflected Mr McMaster's use of earthy language. The chunkie swearbox came complete with a tariff to cover any of Mr McMaster's linguistic lapses. It also had a lock for which the financial controller of Welsh National Opera has the key. Cash raised by the use of offending expletives will go into their funds.

WHEN Viennese conductor Walter Weller was named as the new leader of the Royal Scottish National Orchestra, his reputation came before him. A musician recalled an earlier collaboration with Mr Weller. Before going on stage Mr Weller turned and spat, delicately but still a spit, on the musician's shoulder. This was not an insult, he was pleased to learn, but a venerable Austrian tradition signifying good luck.

DUE to some shameless plugging of jazz by Radio Scotland producer Dave Batchelor, the Diary was plagued with far more banjo jokes than anyone could wish to know:

- How can you tell if there's a banjo player at the door? He can't find the key. Or, he doesn't know when to come in.
- What's the definition of perfect pitch? Throwing a banjo into the lavvy without hitting the seat.
- What's the difference between a macaw and a banjo? One is loud, obnoxious, and noisy. The other is a bird.
- What do you call 25 banjo-players up to their necks in sand? Not enough sand.
- What is the definition of a gentleman? Someone who can play the banjo but doesn't.
- What's the difference between a banjo lying crushed on the road and a hedgehog lying crushed on the road? The hedgehog will have skid marks in front of it.
- What's the difference between

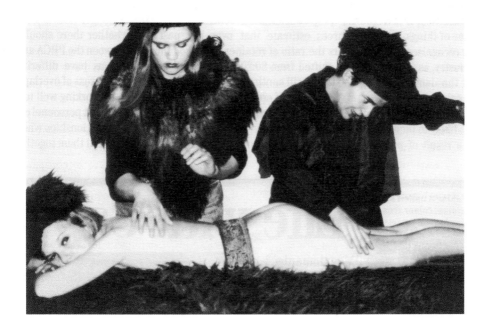

chopping up a banjo and chopping up an onion? No one cries when you chop up a banjo.

- What's the difference between jumping up and down on a banjo and jumping up and down on a trampoline? You take your shoes off to jump up and down on a trampoline.
- What do you call 2,000 banjos thrown into the river Clyde? A good start.
- How many strings does a banjo have? Five too many.
- How do you get two banjo players to play in unison? Shoot one.
- How do you make a banjo player slow down? Put some sheet music in front of him.

THE author William McIlvanney relates a wee story which shows the downside to fame. The scene is a pub in Willie's hame toon o' Kilmarnock, where he is trying to have a quiet drink. Up comes a chap who begins by saying: 'To let you understand, I don't like to interrupt your night but there's somebody wants to meet you.' And there he is at the end of the bar, the man in the raincoat clutching a poly bag full of writing. The man begins by telling McIlvanney that he doesn't actually like his books but he would value an opinion on his own work, which he happens to have with him in the poly bag. 'I'm sorry, I don't have my specs here,' says McIlvanney, patting his left inside jacket pocket. Which is true, since his

38

specs are in his right inside jacket pocket. Undeterred, the would-be author takes a sheaf of paper from his poly bag. Amid the sound of darts, pool, juke boxes, and general bedlam, he leans forward and recites into McIlvanney's ear: 'It was a dark night in Amsterdam. Spencer was dead. There were three possibilities . . .'

AS you no doubt all know, Ravel was the composer who wrote that bit of music for the film *10*. You know, the scene where Dudley Moore and Bo Derek boogie on down. According to the programme for a recent concert by the Royal SNO, it appears there's more stuff like yon *Bolero* in Ravel's repertoire. On the subject of Ravel's *La Valse*, it says: 'For students of Ravel there is the almost unique fascination of hearing the fastidiously antiromantic Ravel gradually unleashing swords of heady romantic passion such as we hardly expect of him. It is as though he were trying to plot the seismography of orgasm on a graph – the orgasm not just of two people but of a whole society that regarded itself as a civilisation.' Which would explain the number of people who left the concert asking: 'And how was it for you, dear?'

ALAN SHARP

AS A successful man of letters, Alan Sharp is doubly exposed to the standard Scottish reaction to the boy who has done good. There is no doubt someone somewhere who will say: 'Alan Sharp? Ah kent baith his faithers.'

Sharp – author of a great Scottish novel, *A Green Tree in Gedde*, and a top-honcho Hollywood scriptwriter – is the seed of Peter Craig, a Dundee communist, and the son of Joe Sharp, a Greenock salvationist. It is, as Sharp says, a genetic web overlaid with a cultural web which he is unpicking to this day.

But first we fast-forward from an Alyth nursing home where in 1934 a Dundee lass is giving birth to her second illegitimate child to a masterclass at the Edinburgh Film Festival in 1992. Sharp is telling his wee tales to an enraptured audience of mainly young film buffs. Like how he was called before a studio boss to discuss an African adventure script which Sharp had begun with a scene where two homosexual Scottish slave traders are playing badminton on the banks of the Limpopo. The studio boss just loved Sharp's writing, but could he not make his characters a bit more

cardboard?

Like when he was working with Peter Fonda and couldn't understand a word the guy was saying until he caught up on the marijuana gap. Sharp has an easy way with the earnest questions. A young lady takes Sharp to task on the fact that he professes an anti-violence stance yet his film *Ulzana's Raid* showed full-frontal

40

Apache torture and mutilation while the film *The Searchers* portrayed the same horror just in John Wayne's face. 'I guess that's because it was a far better movie,' says Sharp. '*The Searchers* was the apogee of the gear.'

As a skilled writer of dialogue, how did Sharp cope with writing so many westerns? 'Well, you just have to get them off their horses and get them talking.' Sharp's first western, *Billy Two Hats*, is shown after the discussion. It features Gregory Peck as a Scottish character who teams up with a half-breed Indian. As the two find themselves surrounded by baddies, Peck has such lines as 'We made a right midden of that' and 'If your auntie had a moustache, she'd be your uncle'. You can take the screenwriter out of Greenock but you can't take Greenock out of the screenwriter.

Or, as a young buff puts it, Sharp remains 'remarkably untainted by Hollywood'. Sharp replies that this is because he was already well tainted by Scotland before he went.

While Sharp was back in Scotland for the Edinburgh Film Festival retrospective of his work, he also completed the first draft of a script for a film about Rob Roy which Peter Broughan of Bronco Films, Glasgow, is trying to process through the movie machine. 'Rob Roy,' says Sharp, 'was just a footnote in Scottish history but he was mixed up with some heavy dudes.' He then goes on to summarise a story of political and economic chicanery in early eighteenth-century Scotland involving the dukes of Montrose and Argyll. As Sharp tells it, Rob Roy was a pretty decent guy whose misfortunes led him into 'outlawry and thievage'.

But in the film process much of this background detail has inevitably to be lost in favour of action. Fortunately, there was plenty as Rob Roy escaped from a foe by plunging off his horse into a Highland river or leaped from a castle turret on to a convenient tree. What we have here is great potential for a Highland western.

During this return to Scotland, Sharp has spoken so much that when he is interviewed he says he feels he is playing a worn-out record. It is a record with many interesting tracks as he fluently addresses such issues as politics, football, sex, drugs, literature and everything. Ask him his views of the state of the Scottish nation after the 1992 general election and his answer begins in Washington DC where the USA is run by a handful of vested interests and lobbyists within the Parkway belt, where the exercise of politics is not governance but the retention of power in a country where 98 per cent of incumbents are re-elected.

Then look at the British system. A televised parliament which 'is Monty Python before our very eyes'. He says: 'My belief is that before you can move towards anything like direct democracy you have to work with smaller constituencies. You cannae do it with 250 million people. You cannae do it with 50 million people but you can wi five million people.'

Which brings us to Scotland. 'Units have to be smaller to permit a more direct democratic process. Scotland was an ideal example. Here was a country, the only country on the planet that could have its independence if it wanted without having to fight for it. They will not send tanks up here. They will do all kinds of other things. And if they don't send tanks, you will not have to find terrorists to fight them. You will not have a government that has been born out of welfare and that's a big plus.'

Sharp takes a pragmatic view of Scotland's historical relationship with England. 'The Scots are a very interesting mob in as much as they made a very interesting deal with the English. A sane deal. It had a lot of problems to it but the alternative was to have these bastards come up here and kick your arse every 25 years.' And, he says, the English have been pretty fair in the sense that they have said: 'Send us your best and brightest and we'll use them. And they've done it and rewarded them by making them prime ministers and the rest.

'The relationship the Scots have to the English is a symbiotic one and giving it up is psychologically very difficult because it's going to take away your excuse. With the English there we can say '"if it wisnae for them bastards" . . . and I've been watching Scottish fitba long enough to understand the Scottish psyche and my own. All the Scots need is an excuse.'

And when it comes to excuses after a Tory general-election win, the Scots have a double whammy. We can blame both the English and the Scottish Labour leaders in whom the voters placed their trust. 'My question is, did the Scots actually believe they were Scottish? Did they actually believe all this stuff they say about themselves? "A man's a man for a' that. The rank is but the guinea stamp." Or was it all just a performance, a fiction with which we maintain ourselves? We all tell ourselves wee stories like we're good in bed or could have been a good midfield player. We usually take care not to put ourselves in a situation where we get called on it.'

If Scotland was too feart to grasp some form of devolution through the ballot box, perhaps it might be just as well to go further down the road of Tory victories, with the hardships involved, to reach some other kind of political solution. It is difficult to make big alterations in a system just by changing where you hold your parliament.

In global as well as Scottish terms, Sharp is a believer in apocalypse soon: 'I am a New Ageist. I believe big shit is coming down in a millennial kinda sense. The truth will set you free but first it will make you fucking miserable. We are looking at hard times all around.'

This seems as good a point as any to change the subject to the relatively cheerful subject of the state of Scottish football. Again Sharp approaches this from a historical perspective. He loves the game but in the

1974 World Cup in Germany experienced a pain that was totally disproportionate to any grown man's expectation.

'I was sickened and yet they played well that year. You'd love to have a Scottish team like that today. By the time Argentina came I was cured. I converted to may the best team win. If it was my team that was a bonus. My problem was that there were getting less and less good games of football in World Cups I've been to. The last one was a fucking travesty. The final was a game I would have walked out of if it had been at Cappielow.'

Sharp would settle for a Scottish team which doesn't win the World Cup but will 'play characteristically well in an over-ornate style, an embellished way of playing the game which is not efficient but is awfy nice to watch. More than entertaining, aesthetically brave. To play the backheel when it would be better to kill the ball and push it to the side. Or hit the through ball that leaves the defender like a quadraplegic. If they ever played a whole game like that it would be incredible, but I'm looking even for a 25-minute spell in the middle. OK if they then say we were only kidding, you can beat us now.'

Before we enter into more personal territories such as life, love, sex, drugs, drink and literature it is useful to have a quick résumé of the life of Alan Sharp. So, meanwhile, back at the nursing home in Alyth in 1934 where Ethel Foot has given birth to a son. It is not certain whether the father, Peter Craig, back in Dundee even knows about the situation.

The baby is adopted at six weeks by Joe and Meg Sharp, working-class Salvation Army people from the Wee Dublin area of Greenock. If Alan Sharp took in his socialism at birth, it was his Greenock upbringing that gave him his way with words.

'Joe Sharp was a profoundly religious man, a Christian man with all the limitations that brings. With a bit more education I'm sure he would have become a minister. The Salvation Army was a more cheerful fundamentalism than, for instance, the Wee Frees.'

Joe Sharp had a penchant for the high-blown phrase, as used in the Salvation Army process of giving testimony and reciting homilies; the wee tales which Sharp describes as his basic craft. But also the aphorisms and lore of working-class Greenock. Young Alan remembers Joe being ticked off by Meg for missing the odd corner when he was distempering the walls. 'Och, a blind man on a galloping horse wouldn't know the difference,' was the reply. Sharp used the line in his western *Billy Two Hats*. He has tried since to introduce it, usually unsuccessfully, into other bits of screenwriting. It now resurfaces as the title of his latest book, a rites-of-passage tale of adolescent life in 1944 Greenock. It will be the first Alan Sharp book in 25 years.

As a young man Sharp worked as a tradesman in the shipyards and as a labourer at IBM. He was going nowhere slowly. At the age of 15 he quit his apprenticeship as a joiner in the yards to be a trainee private-eye after seeing a small ad in the *Greenock Telegraph*. He thought he was going to be Philip Marlowe. The job was as a debt collector. He was back in the yards as a hole-borer within a week. Then he discovered education and literature through the teachers' training scheme which sent him to the yooni and gave him ideas about literature and a realisation of his own talents as a writer. With £500 in his pocket he wanted to take his wife from Greenock to Spain where, in the late 1950s, they could live cheaply and he could be Ernest Hemingway and run with the bulls in Pamplona.

His wife wouldn't go. He gave her the money and left her to find a new life in London, where in the fullness of time he became a writer. The rest of his story is well charted.

He takes his success as a novelist and then as a screenwriter in Hollywood in a matter-of-fact way. 'I'm a talented writer. Not one who's ploughing a bizarre and esoteric furrow but a mainstream writer. I enjoy writing. I just sit down and get on with the tale.' Or to be accurate he used to stand up and get on with the tale. He had an old stand-up desk at which he worked, hand-writing his stories and scripts into bound ledgers. Later in life, at the grand old age of 58, he says he prefers to sit down in a comfortable chair with his ledger in his lap. 'It's so much easier to fall asleep that way.'

Sharp does not conform to the heavy-bevvy stereotype of your Scottish writer. 'I was never a drinker. I drank as part of the rites of passage. I might have been drunk twice in the last few years. I find women a much bigger drug, much more stimulating. Women are the greatest drug of all time; all things are possible.'

Sharp describes his personal relationships as chaotic. Three wives, affairs, love children. He is amazingly frank and open about his personal life. After a career as a serial seducer of women, he is now what you might call a recovering seducer. But when you're a seducer of women, he says, you have to be a placator of women, making up for the lies that are inevitably involved.

'I've only just broken out of that vicious spiral by the simple and old-fashioned thing of stopping fucking around. If you stop you don't have to placate anymore.

'I still look at women the same way but I know that it will all end up in the same place. You can start anywhere you like and go through the romance and the excitement and the passion, the up-the-close part of it. But at the end of the day they'll be looking at you and saying "But you said . . ." and you'll say "What I really meant was . . ." and you're back where you were, so you might as well not start. This isn't wisdom or anything, it's just weariness.'

He lives on the paradise island of Kawau, New Zealand, with Harriet Hall, a black woman from Detroit. 'She's been very helpful to me. She relentlessly called me on my lies, a bit like aversion therapy, until as I sit here there are no more lies.'

One of his remaining addictions is spending a lot of cash on mobility between the different strands of his life in New Zealand, Los Angeles, London and Scotland. He left Los Angeles for New Zealand in 1980. He didn't want to live in Ronald Reagan's America. He wasn't ready to come back to Scotland, didn't fancy Canada or Australia and settled on the provincial fastness of New Zealand.

Sharp has taken to sailing in wee boats. Exposed as he was to the seascape of Greenock as a boy and young man, he never went sailing. That was not for the working classes. In New Zealand it's different, a common hobby like golf is over here. He has an iron-hulled dinghy in which he potters around the Bounty Bar surroundings of the island.

'I've enjoyed learning something new late in life. If I have an aspiration, apart from Scotland winning the World Cup, I would like to sail to Greenock. It would be a long journey and I would need a boat that would allow me to make mistakes but it can be done.'

The old man and the sea. Alan Sharp, still chasing Hemingway after all these years.

RELIGION

A RECURRENT theme in the Diary is bigotry and we were grateful to Pastor Jack Glass for some historical background on the subject. The wee pastor's organ, the *Scottish Protestant View*, contained an article 'Proud to be a bigot' which explained: 'In the days of the stake when Protestants were burned alive by Roman Catholic priests, the reformer was made to wear a yellow garment of shame with devils and flames painted on it . . . The reformer would say: "By God's grace we will not give in to false religion. By God's grace we will stand for Jesus and contend for the faith." Papists started to call them Bi-Godites. Over time it became bigot. This is not a badge of shame for us.'

A RIGHT uplifting wee tract was pressed into the Diary's hands. It is published by the National Bible Society of Scotland who have entitled it *Hope!*. It begins: 'For many people life has no purpose or meaning. The years come and go, bleak without hope. There seems to be no light at the end of the tunnel. One Old Testament writer sums it up like this: It is useless, useless, said the philosopher. Life is useless, all useless. You spend your life working, labouring, and what do you have to show for it? Generations come and generations go, but the world stays just the same. The sun still rises, and it still goes down, going wearily back to where it must start all over again. What has happened before will happen again. What has been done before will be done again. There is nothing new in the whole world.'

(For best effect, it should be read in your best approximation to the cheerful tones of Rikki Fulton's Reverend I.M. Jolly.) At the end of the pamphlet are the words: 'Text from the Good News Bible.'

THE churches in the Western Isles held a Day of Humiliation and Prayer to intercede with the Lord on the vexed subject of the local council's losing £23m in the BCCI bank collapse. The local kirks – Wee, Free, and plain Church of Scotland – were busy praying and humiliating themselves. The Western Isles Council, more usefully, chose that day to hold a committee of inquiry to establish who was at fault for the missing millions. Meanwhile, over in Edinburgh, in an office not totally unadjacent to the financial heart of Scotland, how did moneybrokers R.P. Martin spend the Day of Humiliation and Prayer? R.P. Martin, the very people who acted for the Western Isles Council in the BCCI matter, were holding a Christmas party.

HEAVEN knows the grassy suburbs of Glasgow, such as Castlemilk and Drumchapel, are teeming with enough weans bearing exotic names without our men of the cloth trying to make it worse. We hear of a child who was very nearly christened Pandora by a Glasgow minister. 'What do you wish to call the child?' he asked the proud father. 'Her name's pinned oan her,' the father replied, a touch indistinctly. 'I baptise you, Pandora,' the minister proceeded.

'Naw, naw. Her name's Agnes. See, it's pinned oan tae her shawl,' the parent corrected him.

WE hear that the Rev. Dr Ian Paisley has taken umbrage at one of the Christmas presents received by his wife. He threw out a basket of dried flowers with the words: 'There'll be no pot-pourri in this house.'

THE newsletter of Strathblane Parish Church reported that parishioners have been suffering from break-ins to cars parked at the church. There was an appeal for £400 to install extra lighting to deter the thieves. Appropriately enough, the theme for that Sunday's worship was 'Lighten Our Darkness'.

SECTARIANISM is on the decline but still reverberates in West of Scotland society. How else could you explain the thinking of the pupil at a school in the Pollok area of Glasgow who knocked at the staff-room door and blurted out the news: 'Please, miss. There's a Catholic dog in the playground.'?

O TEMPORA! O mores! O Motherwell! What we are talking about here is the state-of-the-art Catholic first communion ceremony as reported to us recently from Lanarkshire's cathedral city. It appears that the ceremony has become a touch Hollywood. One of the Motherwell poppets, in a white gown that could have been made for *Dynasty*, was making her way back from the altar when she touched a button on her wrist. This activated a microchip which made her tiara twinkle. Another wee communicant lassie apparently arrived at the church in a horse-drawn coach with four page boys. The opinion among some of the older brigade out Motherwell way is that communion chic has gone too far.

PROOF, if any were needed, that the folk of Larkhall are not the Orange fanatics they're made out to be could be found in the recent district council elections. Two of the town's four councillors on Hamilton district are Tims. There is one Protestant and the fourth is a Muslim. Some of the old attitudes persist, however. When Mustaq Ahmed (he's the Muslim, by the way) was first elected he proudly claimed he was the first Asian councillor to represent an all-white ward. 'It's no' white, it's orange,' he was told. In a recent election there were rumours of some dirty fighting. 'You mean they tried to use the racist card?' he was asked. 'No. They were putting it around that my wife is a Catholic.'

BUSINESS

LET it not be said that there is no sense of humour to be found in the Inland Revenue – well, a pretty bizarre imagination at least. The scene for this story is a large tax office in Kingston-upon-Thames. The Revenue was in the process of hiving off a number of jobs from Kingston to Nottingham.

In a brilliant piece of lateral thinking, it was decided to prepare for this exodus by pretending that the staff had already left for Nottingham. The Nottingham Division was separated from the rest of the office.

Doors were erected bearing the name 'Nottingham'. To make the point quite clear, an artist was brought in to paint murals of Sherwood Forest complete with Robin Hood and Maid Marion.

In best Civil Service tradition, a memo was issued to all staff setting out the rules: 'With effect from Monday, 2 March, and until further notice, Sections 4, 5 and 6 are to be regarded for all official purposes as being in Nottingham. No visits for official purposes may be made to those sections by anyone outside the Nottingham Division.

'There is, of course, no ban on unofficial or social visits, though please avoid discussing official matters in the process . . . Official contacts are to be made by telephone or by

memo only . . . Should a visit be unavoidable, a note needs to be made of the reason and the time taken. Allowance should be made for the fact that a return visit from London to Nottingham (and vice versa) would take a day.'

With mind-boggling thoroughness, the Revenue had a system to simulate the 24-hour delay in sending documents from Kingston to Nottingham. 'Items coming into the Nottingham Division will be brought into Sections 4, 5 and 6 in a barrow and left for 24 hours.'

But where there is an emergency, a judicial review or a complaint by an MP 'it may be appropriate to consider a "fax".' To simulate a fax, a Kingston tax officer would walk past the Nottingham section to the messenger section and hand the piece of paper over to a messenger who would then take it to 'Nottingham'.

At this point the rules suffered an unwelcome attack of common sense. 'Staff will be expected to use their discretion when exceptional circumstances arise . . . The excuse that the office was "pretending to be in Nottingham" would sound pretty thin if it caused an additional delay.'

ANYTHING is fair game these days for the ubiquitous newspaper advertising supplement. But perhaps the *Aberdeen Press and Journal* was pushing matters a bit by inviting advertisers to buy their way into a supplement to 'celebrate the 300th anniversary of the massacre of Glencoe'. One chap who certainly thought so was Mr Rob MacDonald Parker, director of the Clan Donald Centre on Skye, given that the MacDonalds of Glencoe, victims of the bloody murders, were his kith and kin. He received a letter inviting his tourist attraction to pay for advertising space in this celebratory supplement. He was not impressed. Particularly since the letter was signed by a *Press and Journal* advertising executive by the name of Adrian Campbell.

ACCOUNTANCY isn't the most exciting way of life. For instance, when was the last time you heard of a youngster running away to join Ernst & Young? But a bold move by Colonel John Blashford-Snell, the man behind Operation Raleigh, could change all this. He issued this chal-

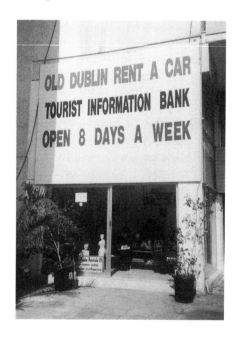

50

lenge to chartered accountants: 'Operation Raleigh, the organisation that gives young people a taste of adventure and leadership on ventures worldwide, is looking for short-term secondees from accounting profession to act as field accountants on its expeditions. Volunteers would be sent to expedition locations to carry out usual accounting and liaison with local banks, businesses, and sponsors as well as Raleigh headquarters, up to preparing final accounts . . .'

The Diary managed to get hold of the chief accountant's report on a recent Operation Raleigh expedition to the North Pole:

- *Leith, 21 March:* The team set sail in good spirits. Managed to sell the ship to a Hong Kong company and negotiate a lease-back on very favourable terms. Have high hopes of reaching the Pole and making a profit.

- *Cape Farewell, Greenland, 20 April:* Disaster. Our insolvency expert was washed overboard this morning, leaving only myself, three trainee accountants, two secretaries, four book-keepers, and a data-systems manager for the arduous task ahead.

- *Ellesmere Island, 3 May:* Our first base camp. Our IBM computers are working well despite the freezing cold. Would like to take the entire accounts department all the way to the Pole but Colonel Blashford-Snell says there is no room on the sled. Will have to put the spreadsheets on to a lap-top and hope for the best.

- *Fifty miles from the Pole, 12 July:* Sixteen of the young explorers have died of frostbite. One of the team leaders blames it on my decision back in Leith to cut the clothing budget by 50 per cent. He doesn't seem to understand the need for

51

tight cost control. Point out that the wastage rate in young explorers, in fact, compares favourably with previous expeditions.

- *Twenty-five miles from Pole, 3 August:* A bitter blow. My book-keeper plunged to her death down a ravine, taking the lap-top with her. Luckily I had the double-entry ledger in my rucksack at the time.
- *Five miles from the Pole, 10 August:* Farquhar, our last trainee accountant, is suffering from severe frostbite after an all-night session working without gloves on a very tricky VAT problem. Says he is now just a hindrance to the accounts department and walks out into the blizzard saying he is off 'to make a final reconciliation and may be some time'. Have written to Edinburgh recommending him for the Institute of Chartered Accountants' highest award.
- *North Pole, 15 August:* Colonel Blashford-Snell raises a Union Jack at the Pole. Use my ice-axe to bury a copy of the interim accounts. Feel the expedition has been most interesting but long to be back at my desk in Glasgow implementing some exciting new Compliance Review Techniques into our standard audit procedures in response to the latest round of Companies Act legislation.

A TRUE story of a chartered accountant on holiday in France who took his family to visit a cathedral. 'Daddy,' said number-one son, who was obviously set to follow in the true (accounting) faith, 'what are all these plus signs doing everywhere?'

NORMAN

WEDNESDAY, 16 September 1992 has joined my personal pantheon of 'where were you when . . . ?' Like: where were you when you heard JFK had been shot? (I was collecting window-cleaning money for Alfie McLaughlin, shammy-artist of Priesthill, Glasgow.) Or: where were you when you heard Mo Johnston had signed for Rangers? (Having lunch at an international conference on jurisprudence at Glasgow University, but I left sharpish to interview the denizens of sundry bluenose pubs at Bridgeton Cross.)

So, where was I on so-called Black Wednesday, the day of sterling chaos? The day Norman Lamont, in a vain effort to defend the pound, put the interest rate up five per cent. Then he indulged in Eurocurrency interruptus. Then, to cap a perfect day, he was photographed amid the dustbins as he tried to sneak out of the Treasury by the back door. The day which prompted the *Sun* headline writer to pen: 'Now we've all been screwed by the Cabinet'. Actually I was in the middle of the action, with a front seat in the Royal Bank of Scotland dealing room in the City.

The Royal Bank had kindly co-operated in my mission to understand by letting me sit in at their treasury and capital markets division in London. Senior dealer Fergie Buchan was explaining some details of the foreign exchange market, specifically how he had made a few shillings for Royal Bank customers that morning by taking a position on the mark versus the yen.

Fergie had started to describe the torrent of money that was getting out of sterling and into stronger currencies when there came news of the first two per cent interest-rate rise. I waited for the activity in the dealing room to become even more frantic. Why no frantic activity, I asked Fergie. Why no sudden improvement in the pound? 'The two per cent will make no difference. The speculators are still chucking sterling at the Bank of England,' he said.

How come that Fergie, a self-taught foreign exchange dealer, knew this but Mr Lamont and his high-powered team at the Treasury and Bank of England didn't? Fergie said: 'The market's been telling the Chancellor that a realignment or devaluation of sterling is needed, but he's not been listening.'

Three hours later Mr Lamont is maybe starting to listen. He puts the bank rate up a further three per cent and this time elicits a response. It is from a dealer in interest-rate futures I meet in the pub downstairs. He has pulled out of the market for the moment, having made a nice wee profit in the morning. 'I don't know what's happening. Most of the people I do business with don't know what's happening. The Bank of England doesn't know what's happening. Least of all Norman Lamont knows what's happening.'

We've all heard the stories. The manager of a broker's firm who pointed to the lads on his dealing floor and said proudly: 'Not an O-level among them but you should see them make money . . .' A Scots girl working in advertising in London and stepping out with one of the Essex dealer lads told me simply: 'Beasts. They're all beasts.' And this from someone who grew up in Airdrie.

This analysis is certainly not borne out by my brief encounter with the lads in the Royal Bank dealing room. Perhaps because they have a healthy leavening of Scots. Fergie Buchan, who was born in Broughty Ferry and saw service in Banff and various branches of the Royal Bank, has not so much embraced the lifestyle of the Jack-the-Lad Home Counties banker as taken them on at their own game.

He tells you with a broad grin that he lives at Pratts Bottom in Kent. Near Badgers Mount. He's up at five thirty a.m. to be at his City desk for

seven a.m. After a long day, there's maybe time to squeeze in a couple of pints before getting home at nine p.m. Even if he is occasionally called into the office at eleven thirty p.m. from his local, his is one of the more relaxed regimes. He and his colleagues could have tripled their salaries by leaving the relative peace and quiet of his clearing bank for one of the more zoo-like dealing rooms. Big bonuses; fast burnout.

A run of bad deals and your P45 is in the post. The Royal Bank is more forgiving. 'If a dealer is on a bad run, he can put his hands up and be taken out of the front line until he finds his form again. We have a management system which prevents dealers chasing their losses.' A sensible precaution in a business which previously had seen two dealers in Adam & Co., the small Scottish bank, rack up losses of £21m.

Not that the Royal Bank boys are any kind of wimps. One of the dealers has put on his hat with the rubber horns. He is feeling bullish and is on a good run. There are outbreaks of hand-slapping as the business is being done.

Fergie was explaining his work ethic: 'I'm in and out like a ratcatcher's dog. Grab the profit and get out.' Warming to the theme, he explained the current philosophy of the foreign-exchange market towards the lira, sterling, and other weak currencies: 'We smelled blood and we went for the throat.'

At this point the nice man who was tailing me from the Royal Bank public relations began to look concerned. Fergie moderated this to: 'In this business you've got to go with the crowd. We've got to look after our customers. Only 20 per cent of our transactions is speculation by the bank.

'Most of the business we do is commercial work for our customers.' With so much going on that day, it didn't seem the right time to ask questions such as why do we need so many people buying and selling foreign currency when they're not even going on holiday.

Luckily there is a book on the subject published, appropriately, by the Swiss Bank Corporation. It explains that foreign exchange dealings spring from 'the coexistence between the internationalism of trade and the nationalism of currencies'. It's all in there – spot dealings, futures, long and short positions with handy wee examples. In 92 simple-to-follow pages, you too can learn to be a foreign-exchange dealer. The book concludes: 'That's it! Once you've digested all this, you will have the technical knowledge to be a foreign-exchange dealer. Even if there is some truth to the saying that foreign-exchange dealers are not made, they are born, don't get discouraged.'

Fergie Buchan described the essence of the whole business more succinctly: 'Buy cheap, sell dear.' Some dealers have refined their work to roaming the system electronically in the hope of finding a fellow dealer who has made a mistake by setting too favourable a rate and then ripping him off. It is no wonder that there has been the occasional 'ruck', as the Essex lads call it, in the pub after a day's dealing.

So who are the speculators? The Bank of America did their image no good by having one of their dealers admit on ITN news that they had made £10m profit on that wacky Wednesday.

The central bank of one of the Far East countries is famous among dealers for its predatory style. Far from being a force for calm, as a central bank is supposed to be, this bank has a $100 billion war chest which it uses to wage war on ailing currencies. There are also the wealthy individuals who sit at home with the same electronic kit as the dealers and move their cash around for profit but also pleasure in a high-stakes parlour game. But the bad news for idealists is that the speculators are . . . you and me. Our insurance companies, our banks, our unit trusts, probably even the firm we work for. When the rush out of sterling was at its peak that Tuesday and Wednesday, some of Britain's blue-chip companies were at the head of the queue.

One of the fascinating aspects of the money market is the obscure reasons analysts come up with to explain movements in currencies. When the market was talking down sterling there were a few beauties like nervousness caused by the floating of the Finnish markka. Or a fall in the USA non-farm payroll index.

Scott Bannister, the Royal Bank's futures manager and another canny Scot who went to their City office after shuffling pesetas at the foreign currency counter in a Glasgow branch, said: 'Indicators go in and out of fashion. Money supply used to be popular then it got boring. US non-farm payrolls is a favourite at the moment. On my screen at the moment is a headline from Reuters telling us that US business inventories are up 0.1 per cent. Is that good news

because American firms are stocking up for good times ahead? Or bad news because American firms can't shift their products? Take your pick.

'I often feel that after something has happened on the market, people look for something to blame.'

Among the information supplied by Reuters to the dealers that afternoon was the fact that President Mitterrand was suffering from prostate cancer. One of the lads was heard later wondering aloud how 'Mitterrand's willie trouble' will affect the market.

The Swiss Bank Corporation's bible admits that currency dealing is less than an exact science: 'Psychological factors can also have a bearing on exchange-rate behaviour, mainly by inducing capital flows. In this connection it is noteworthy that many currencies have a certain image; the Swiss franc has the image of a refuge currency which explains at least part of its inherent strength; in turbulent times it is often such images, rather than any solid reason, which make people move in and out of certain currencies.'

So there we have it. Our lives and mortgages ruled by US non-farm payrolls, Mitterand's willie problem, and the state of the Finnish markka. For the state of the currency market is beginning to dominate our whole lives. Even on Radio 1 news we hear financial experts rabbiting on about the lira. The vicar on the morning service on Radio 4 the other day asked us to pray to God for a stable currency and asked God to guide Norman Lamont.

The money-market fever was even affecting some cherished British institutions the day I was in the City. Over a cooling pint of Tennent's Pilsener, as the stuff is called down there, I was listening to a collection of suits discuss the day's events. 'Bloody 15 per cent,' said one. 'The Tories will have to go. It's time we had a bloody revolution!'

Pigs might fly. And the lira might rise.

MAXWELL

GRIEF was not universal among Robert Maxwell's employees when news came through that the great publisher had fallen from his yacht and drowned. In the *Daily Record* building in Glasgow the day after the drowning and with Maxwell's body as yet unrecovered, there was in circulation a map of the Canary Islands with a grid superimposed. For £1 a shot you could indulge in a game of chance called Spot the Bob.

A GROUP of *Daily Record* employees celebrated Maxwell's demise with an anniversary lunch. The main course was seafood with Sticky Fingers Pudding for dessert.

THE mystery of Maxwell's last hours was explained when it was revealed that he had gone on the cruise on doc-

tor's orders. 'Take a break,' the doc told him. 'Relax. Have a few good meals and a few drinks. But don't go overboard.'

WHEN Maxwell took out a libel action against *Private Eye*, he attracted much awe-struck sympathy by bursting into tears in the witness box as he recalled his family being wiped out at Auschwitz by the Nazis. He was awarded £55,000 damages. This rang a bell with a member of the *Scottish Daily News* co-operative who remembered a stormy mass meeting at which Maxwell was under fire for grabbing power at the newspaper. A voice from the back of the hall shouted, 'Fascist'. Maxwell duly burst into tears and pleaded: 'How can you say that when my family was wiped out at Auschwitz by the Nazis?' There was an awkward, almost respectful silence. Then another irreverent Glesca voice shouted: 'Ah bet ye shopped them, ya bastard.'

POLY

THE swan-like transformation of sundry polytechnics into universities was the subject of some ribaldry in the Diary. A particular target was the Glasgow Caledonian University which, even in its days as Glasgow College of Technology, was referred to as the University of Coocaddens. This was because the upstart educational establishment had delusions of grandeur and kept changing its name in attempts to go upmarket.

Now life has overtaken fiction and Glasgow Polytechnic, as the college was known for a few years, has the status of university. But the search for a suitable name was not without tribulation. The first choice was City University but Mr Norman Thompson, a founding but now former member of the staff of the illustrious educational establishment, wrote: 'I would seriously counsel against the adoption of the title City University . . . In a city which abhors pomposity and responds to it actively, the title "city" would be all too easily mispronounced.' There were some serious suggestions such as Buchanan University, after the former train-station site on which the college is built, but these were quickly ignored.

We discovered that entry qualifications to Glasgow's third yoonie were stricter than we thought and not merely having to quote your mother's Co-op number. Two set books must be completed – one fully coloured in (without going over the lines) and the other with all the dots joined up. The poly also demands mathematical proficiency to the standard of undertaking long division together with proven ability to 'carry one' in hard sums.

The poly's aspiration to be called Queen's University, Glasgow, was kicked into touch and they then went for Glasgow Merchants University. This was soon amended on campus to the Patter Merchants University, the Bevvy Merchants University, and the Scrap Merchants University. Another alternative suggestion is that the new yoonie be called the Gardner Merchant University after the esteemed catering company which has the contract to feed the staff. The concept of the Merchants University was quickly dropped.

A study of the 1828 David Smith map of the Cowcaddens showed that there had once been a lunatic asylum on the site of Glasgow's third yoonie. This institution was the Magdalene

Asylum, giving a precedent for the elegant Magdalene College, Glasgow. Or the inelegant Looney Yoonie. Another idea was that the proximity of the campus to the old Normal School led naturally to the Normal University. There was a school of thought that this was an ideal opportunity to commemorate that great thinker Duns Scotus. So how about Dun Larnin University or even Dunstudian Yoonie?

Another serious suggestion was University of Caledonia, prompted by the fact that the stockyards of the railway of that name once occupied the site. And this obviously struck a chord, with Glasgow Caledonian University the actual name chosen by a ballot paper of staff and students. The successful title was thus described in a news release: 'Glasgow Caledonian University – The title is pronounceable and distinctive both in its full form and in its acronym. This title abbreviates easily, e.g. Cally, Cal-U (as in the American form).' This led to speculation of such snippets of overheard conversation as 'I'm at the Cally Yoonie' or 'Yes, Farquhar's doing awfy well. He's majoring in bulk solids handling at Cal-U. No, not Los

Angeles, the wan in the Coocaddens.'

The blurb continued: 'The images associated with Caledonian are used in marketing worldwide to evoke trust, integrity, and a quality of life worth seeking.'

But the ribaldry was not over for poor Glasgow Caledonian University. Instead of abbreviating to Cal-U, it was generally felt more likely that it would be shortened to CU. Which has an altogether different meaning, Jimmy. And it was not long before people were suggesting it should have been called Caledonian MacBrain University.

SCHOOL

THE Use of Language and That: A new teacher at Annan Academy (a young lady from south of the border) was appalled to see a fourth-year boy running full pelt along the main corridor at four p.m. She stopped him and asked why he was running. 'I'm trying to catch the 'Fechan bus,' he replied. She promptly doled out a one-hour detention for his use of foul language. Which is why the lad was so late getting home to Ecclefechan.

FROM examination papers from a school in deepest Ayrshire we can pass on to youse such information as:

- The capital of Scotland is S.
- The highest mountain in Scotland is Ben Everest.
- Wanlockhead is similar to Leadhills . . . and they both have minefields around them.
- The Sahara is a hot dessert.

FROM the news book of a Govan primary-school pupil: 'Emperor Hirohito had a very big funeral. It took 50 men to carry the beer.'

TWO fresh-faced five-year-olds found themselves involved in a playground fight in their first week at school. The boy on top finally tired of administering a right doing and enquired of his opponent: 'Have you had enough?' 'I don't know,' replied the other. 'This is my first fight.'

ONE of the more delicate problems teachers have to deal with is when a pupil is deficient in the Lifebuoy department. One teacher was compelled to take wee Jimmy aside and impart some advice on personal hygiene. The next day Jimmy's irate mother confronted the teacher with the statement: 'Ma son's in school tae be telt, no' smelt.' She added a scrap of information which did not come as news to the teachers: 'He's no' an effan' geranium.'

GREAT School Absence Notes of Our Time: A teacher at a well-known penal institution (aka school) in the deep south-west of Glasgow swears genuinely to have received the following parental missive: 'Dear Sir, Please excuse John for being absent as he spewed up the whole of Peat Road.'

The text of another absence note was not all that unusual. The missive from wee Jimmy's mum was of a stan-

dard variety, stating that he had been awfy no' well and had been kept off the school. What struck the teacher was that the note was well crumpled and looked as if the mother had picked up any old scrap of paper she could find. Indeed she had. When the teacher turned the scrap of paper over she found another message reading: 'Your dinner's in the oven. If you want sex later, just wake me up . . .'

The letter from a mother explaining her wee boy's non-attendance was graphic and to the point: 'Dear Miss, Sorry Peter isn't at school. I gave him syrup of figs last night. He hasn't been yet, but when he goes, he'll come.'

FROM the Mouths of Babes: The cast of the nativity play at St Joseph's playgroup, Clarkston, were busy rehearsing their lines. Imagine the scene. The three wise men have followed the star and have reached the stable. 'I bring gold,' says the first wise bairn. 'I bring myrrh,' says the second. The concept of frankincense is proving difficult for the third wee wise man as he offers hopefully: 'I'll just bring the sandwiches.'

THIS from an anonymous schoolteacher in a primary school of Catholic origins in the South Side of Glasgow which goes to great pains to encourage non-diocesan children to attend. The weans are looking forward to the advent of Christmas. The principal is helping set up the stable scene with Mary, Jesus, and Joseph, the three Kings, some lowing cattle et al. While thus engaged he is approached by a child of a non-Catholic denomination. 'Sir,' the child asks, looking at the plethora of straw in the manger, 'Does the school keep hamsters?'

A PUPIL at a Lanarkshire primary school returned home after a sex education lesson so well versed in the subject that he was able to tell his parents that 'boys have got a penis and girls have got a fat china'.

HEALTH

WITH staff cutbacks and inadequate resources, life is difficult for the nurses in Glasgow's hospital casualty units. It is not surprising, therefore, that some nurses take a hard line with the various down-and-outs who feign illness to obtain a bed for the night. One such sister in a hospital which shall remain nameless has perfected a technique whereby she approaches a patient suspected of pretending to be unconscious and grabs him firmly by the family jewels. She was called upon to use her skills recently by a young doctor who was unsure about the genuineness of a patient. Hearing the resulting screams, the doctor returned to the scene with the words: 'No, sister, not him. The man in the next cubicle.'

A GENTLEMAN from Bishopbriggs was in Stobhill Hospital for a vasectomy. He was awaiting this routine operation in a room with a number of other chaps, all of whom became slightly alarmed when a young nursing auxiliary came in clutching a cardboard box and asked the sister: 'What do you want done with these balls?' The box contained, of course, Christmas decorations.

AN apocryphal tale concerns Mr John Cockburn, an eminent surgeon at Aberdeen Royal Infirmary cardiac unit. He was guest speaker at a function run by a pharmaceutical company in Edinburgh and during the meal the company's young English representative kept referring to him as Cock-burn. 'It's Co'burn, as in the film actor,' John told him. The rep, by this time very nervous, kept repeating to himself as the time drew near to introduce the surgeon's speech 'It's Co'burn, Co'burn' then promptly stood up to introduce John Heartburn, the respected cock surgeon.

A YOUNG man was proudly relating to his mother how he was on the nicotine patches and had given up smok-

ing. His mum inspected the patch and recommended: 'What you should do is put on all the patches and get that nicotine out of your system in the one go.'

THE concept behind the nicotine patches quickly caught on. There were reports of a chap going around with a teabag taped to his arm who said he was trying to give up tea. Not to mention the man with a pie on his arm to see if he could lose weight.

THE Body Shop factory in Easterhouse, Glasgow, where they make the designer soap, is one of the more desirable workplaces in the area. As you would expect from the principles established by founder Anita Roddick, everything involved is of the best. Workers are encouraged to pursue a healthy lifestyle by having access to quantities of the Body Shop lotions and ungents. The factory itself is of the modern times variety with designer overalls. An industrial paradise you

would think and you would be right. Apart from one issue raised at a management–staff meeting 'Everything's fine,' said one chap, 'but could we not have white rolls instead of those brown ones in the canteen?'

SPORT

THE Diary's attention was drawn to strange signs in two municipal swimming pools. Glasgow's North Woodside Leisure Centre, the old Woodside Baths as was, had been refurbished in ancient-Roman style. The authorities, perhaps concerned that orgies may occur in such a setting, have put up a sign which includes among its prohibitions the words: 'No petting'. To reinforce the

point, the sign is illustrated by a cartoon in which a well-endowed lady swimmer is saying to her male companion: 'No, I don't want to see your breast stroke.' Meanwhile, over in doucest Giffnock, the Eastwood pool has a sign which boldly states: 'Please don't pee in our pool. We don't swim in your toilet.' More appropriate to the area, we thought, is the sign in the shower area headed 'Protection of privacy' which urges swimmers to keep their swimwear on in the showers to avoid embarrassing others.

OUR reference to the *defense de pisser dans le pool* sign at Eastwood baths brought a rejoinder from Austin Lafferty of Pollokshields (one of the Diary's regular correspondents, now sadly deceased). He recalled the occasion when a man was being ejected from a Glasgow swimming baths. Why for?, he asked the attendant. 'For peeing in the pool,' he was told. 'But other people pee in the pool,' he protested. 'Aye, but no' aff the dale,' the attendant replied.

MR Lafferty also took us back to his boyhood in Perth in the 1930s. 'It was before the days of recycling of water in the baths. The baths were filled every Monday, Wednesday and Friday morning from the nearby lake. Monday, Wednesday and Friday were described as fresh-water days, the admission charge being thruppence. Tuesday, Thursday and Saturday were known as dirty-water days, and the charge (dysentery compris) was only tuppence. But at the end of a dirty-water day the contents of the baths resembled something like lentil soup, but without its flavour. It wasn't helped by a practice we boys indulged in. In the shower we were wont to lather our whole selves with the aid of the blocks of carbolic soap thoughtfully provided. Then, to the manifest horror of the attendant, do a 'soapy dive', leaving a submarine trail like Halley's Comet. Eventually the attendant would call you over, and, on enquiry, you said you had fully enjoyed the pleasure of the pool for a quarter of an hour. He was seldom persuaded and insisted on inspection of your fingers which, after a couple of hours, were so furrowed and bleached (by the chlorine and urine) that you had no defence.' Happy days. Insanitary days, but happy days.

DOCTOR John Macpherson, a Dundonian now in exile as a GP in deepest Troon, weighed in with some Dundonian swimming-baths lore. 'The old Central baths are sorely missed. The second-class pool was known to turn from blue to red at about five p.m. every day during the summer. The reason for this was not any decree from the ruling Labour Party but berry juice washing off the schoolkids who had been "at the berries" that day.'

Social historians may be interested to note the phrase 'second-class pool'. The first-class pool was more expensive and a service to those who were prepared to pay a premium to avoid contact with Clootie City's great unwashed.

WE thought the following excerpt from *Wavelength*, the Scottish yachtmaster broadsheet, essential reading for Diary readers who find themselves cast adrift on the ocean waves. It is described as 'a brief description of position fixing while on the move by the principle of dead reckoning . . . written in simplified form'.

It couldn't be simpler: 'Dead reckoning can tell you where you are at any given time, and it operates on the principle that if you know where you were, and if you know where you have gone, then by extrapolating from where you were and where you have gone you can calculate where you are, or at least where you were when you originally started calculating. Since the position where you are now is not the position that you calculated, and the position that you were in then is not the position you are in now, it follows that you have introduced the error. (This is defined as the difference between where are you and where you aren't, but calculated you should be.)'

Stick with us; not long now: 'This

error can be minimised by calculating your next position from the position where you weren't but calculated you were, to the position that you now aren't, because you had just moved. Unfortunately, you still have an error but by this method it does not compound itself, giving rise to an accurate position of where you are not.'

Unfortunately, matters now begin to get complicated: 'If the wind and tide are not equal and opposite then a calculation must be made which takes into account their cumulative force and direction. It is important to remember, however, that the time interval is the time from where you were to where you no longer are. This calculation results in a correction that is to be applied to the position where you are not in order to accurately ascertain that you still are not. Apparently this is the same method as used by Christopher Columbus when he set out to establish the existence of Australasia but discovered the Americas.' Or to simplify matters, where Columbus went wrong was when he reached the Canary Islands. He turned right and ended up in America. For Australia, he should, of course, have gone straight on, first left at the bottom of Africa and straight on past India.

SOMETIMES the Diary became deeply philosophical and asked serious meaning-of-life questions like: Is Ally McCoist really the Greatest Living Ranger? Is Jim McLean really God? How long could Terry Cassidy get away with it at Celtic Park?

We were saved from the much simpler debate: What is sport? when the Sports Council issued their Research Document No. 21 on this very subject: 'It was necessary to define clearly the concept of sport . . . This includes all activities which might be popularly recognised as sport . . . but excludes greyhound racing in which animals are the only active participants.' (The Sports Council chaps have obviously never been to Shawfield or Powderhall on a race night.)

The report continues: 'Popular physical activities such as dancing, snooker, billiards, pool, and walking (two or more miles for leisure purposes) are also included in this definition, but the game of darts is not included.'

So, there you have it. A chap who walks two miles from his house in Maryhill to a disco in town, meets Senga for a spot of dancing, and walks her home has been doing sport. (No, we don't know if aerobic winching counts as sport.) The chap who stayed in the pub playing darts cannot be counted a sportsman but the guy next to him playing pool in the smoky confines of the boozer has been doing sport.

WISDOM, Weans, From the Mouths of: It appears that in our schools even jolly old PE has been blighted with academic jargon. No longer can gym teachers allow the bairns to go out to the playing fields and knock a ball about in the name of sport. Now that the pupils can do an O-level (or whatever the hell it is they're called nowadays) in gym, they have to be learnt proper. Thus we hear of one lady gym teacher trying to inculcate some O-grade hockey into her girls. As she demonstrated a few bits of hockey magic, she asked the class: 'Now what skill is this?' To which one replied: 'North Kelvinside, miss.'

THE British Amateur Gymnastics Association lost out when Coca-Cola withdrew as sponsors of their major awards scheme. But the good news was that the void was filled by Pedigree Pet Foods Ltd. Pedigree chose to name the award scheme after its Kit-E-Kat brand. Neat, don't you think, with the comparisons between agile felines and supple gymnasts? But we felt that Mr Tony Murdock, the association's awards director, took things too far. He stated in a circular on the new sponsorship: 'We sincerely hope that all of our current gymnasts who use the awards will support the sponsor and, hopefully, try out Kit-E-Kat cat food in the coming months.'

FROM darkest Midlothian came a tale which illustrates what a trusting lot bowlers are. Loanhead Miners Welfare were drawn to play Rosslyn at the neutral venue of Rosewell bowling club. To save travelling, it was agreed over a telephone call between the respective skips to play the match at either Loanhead or Rosslyn. 'Where will we meet to toss the coin?' asked

the Loanhead man. 'Let's do it over the phone. I'll trust you,' replied the Rosslyn man. 'OK, call.' 'Heads.' 'Sorry, it's tails.' We can't see it catching on in less trustworthy pairts than Midlothian.

WORLD boxing champion Walter McGowan, explaining how he came to be a hungry fighter, described his upbringing in Burnbank, a garden suburb of Hamilton: 'It was the jungle in Burnbank that we came from. You had to sleep with your socks on if you wanted them in the morning. Pitbull terriers had to run about in pairs up there.'

THE Diary attracted a number of golf jokes of uncertain vintage, like the story of an enthusiastic but inexperienced American who hacked his way around the Old Course in 170 strokes. He confessed to his caddie: 'Gee, I'm so dispirited I could jump into that ol' Swilcan Burn and drown myself.' 'Dinnae bother,' the caddie replied. 'I don't think ye could keep your heid doon lang enough.'

A WILLING but wanting lady golfer on a Kilmarnock municipal course was experiencing great difficulty making contact with the ball. After her third fresh-air shot, she turned to the party of schoolboys who were waiting their turn and apologised for the delay. 'That's all right, missus,' one boy replied. 'We started our school holidays today.'

A MEMBER of an Ayrshire club was playing a round with his wife. He drove his ball into a wooden shelter at the sixth hole. He was about to take a penalty drop when his wife pointed out that two of the planks of wood were missing, providing a slim but tempting chance of pitching to the green which was visible through the aperture. He attempted the shot. Unfortunately, he missed the gap and the ball rebounded fiercely, hitting his dear wife on the forehead, and killing her stone dead. Some six weeks later, having overcome the grief, he was playing the same course with a friend. His drive at the sixth ended up in the same wooden shelter. He declared that he would be taking a penalty drop shot. His partner pointed out that there were two planks missing and he

could possibly chip through and on to the green. 'Oh, no,' he said. 'I tried that before and it was a disaster.' 'What happened?' 'I scored a nine.'

A TRUE story about the golfer who was practising his short iron shots in the privacy of his own back garden. As he practised with his eight-iron, his wife's beloved Yorkshire terrier ran through his legs, making a perfect connection with his downward swing. The poor wee thing was sent flying through the air. We would like to tell you about the powers of the recovery of the Yorkie but the truth is it was dead on arrival at the vet.

Also true and in equally bad taste: An aged member's last request was that his ashes be spread on the eighteenth green. The club captain, charged with carrying out the request, did a less than perfect job. He simply up-ended the urn, leaving Old Tam's remains in a rather large pile on the green, hoping that the breeze would disperse them. Walking back to the clubhouse, he looked back to see that a ball had landed on Old Tam's ashes. The player duly lifted his ball, licked it clean, placed it clear of the obstruction and carried on putting.

STRANGER than fiction are the rules which various golf clubs invent to torment lady visitors. This experience from a woman who accompanied a male friend to Old Ranfurly Golf Club in Bridge of Weir: 'The problem arose in the bar. Drink in hand, I surveyed the room and decided that the best place to sit was near the window where the players could be seen. As I walked towards a vacant table, my companion was asked by the barmaid to call me back to the bar. There, I was informed in embarrassed tones that ladies were not allowed to step off the carpet. The wooden floor was apparently the men's games area. No dividing screens were evident. I enquired from the embarrassed barmaid whether this rule was to stop high heels damaging the hard floor. No, she replied, ladies are just not allowed to step off the carpet area.'

WE were pleased to report a small but significant backlash on the subject of dress codes in golf clubs. Lochwinnoch Golf Club is part of a darts league which includes various local hostelries. When the players from another team turned up at the clubhouse wearing (*quel horreur!*) denims and trainers, they were snootily received by some members. In revenge, when the golf-club chaps paid their return visit to the other team, a sign was prominently displayed with the words: 'No Pringles allowed.'

IT appears that Canadian golfers are more laid back than us about the business of clubhouse rules. A club in Sicamous, British Columbia, has a sign which warns: 'No spikes on dance floor.'

GOLFERS have to fill in those fallow winter months somehow. Some of

the chaps at Williamwood, the select club on the South Side of Glasgow, decided to have a night during which a bird would be hired to get her tits out for the lads, as the current slang vulgarly has it. The performance in which the lady would be engaged to doff her garments purely in the pursuit of the lively arts was to take place in lockfast premises to avoid offence to the innocent. A member of staff, spotting the arrival of a lady ('a right darling' according to an eye-witness) in a fur coat and black stockings guided her into a sideroom and said that she could leave her gear in there while she performed next door. The said member of staff quickly discovered that this is a surefire way of upsetting a member's wife.

FROM the world of horse-racing we heard the Runyonesque tale of Tam, an OAP who goes to Hamilton races with only a tenner. He puts the lot on his choice for the first race which duly romps home at big odds. He puts his winnings on an outsider in the second race which also wins. By the time the last race comes, Tam has £40,000 in his pocket. Being a true punter he puts the lot on the favourite, a horse called Lucky Tam. It is beaten in a photo-finish. He goes home to the wife who asks how he fared. 'No' bad,' he replies. 'I only lost a tenner.'

ANOTHER tale of a superstitious punter who went to bed one night and dreamed all night long about bread – crusty loaves, sliced, pan, plain. The next morning, consulting his *Herald* racing pages, he was delighted to find a nag called Mother's Pride which was a cert for the 3.15 race at Hamilton. He went straight to the bookies and placed £500 on the horse. Returning to collect his certain winnings, he was disgusted to hear from a delighted bookie that the race had, in fact, been won 'by a big outsider'.

RUGBY

GORDON Brown, Broon frae Troon (or Brown from Trown as he became known since his vowels changed slightly after becoming a star on English TV) has so many tales and anecdotes, we hope he doesn't mind us pinching a few. Like the one about referee Allan Hosie officiating at a towsy match between West of Scotland and Langholm. Brian Gossman, of West, tried to nip down the blind side of the scrum to be met by one Langholm player who got him in a neck-breaking hold, while another opponent punched him in the face and indicated that if he tried the ploy again it would be met with even stiffer punishment.

Gossman said to referee Hosie: 'Did you hear that?' The ref indicated that he had. 'Well?' asked Gossman. Hosie replied: 'If I were you I wouldn't go down the blind side again.'

SOME years ago, after a club match away from home, Broon discovered that his car had been moved from where he had parked it, a practical joke in vogue at the time. He returned to the bar and announced, loudly and aggressively, that if the blighters (or a word similar) responsible did not return his car pronto, he would have to do the same as he had done at Hawick two weeks before.

Given Broon's substantial presence, not to mention menace, the car was promptly located. 'By the way,' asked the club secretary of Broon. 'What did you do at Hawick two weeks ago?'

'I had to get a lift home,' said Broon sweetly.

THE post-match Rugby World Cup wake in the pubs of Rose Street on the Saturday night after England beat Scotland at Murrayfield to win the Grand Slam was, for once, even more depressing than the game itself. Cope, if you can, with hordes of English celebrating by drinking half-pints of lager shandy and interminably singing *Swing Low, Sweet Chariot*.

The kilts in the Cafe Royal did their level best to retaliate with a song the lyrics of which they had obviously commissioned from Sammy Cahn or Johnny Mercer. It went: 'You can stick your f****** chariots up your arse.'

US chaps on the Diary do not approve of violence but we could not

help but smile when we were appraised of this overheard conversation in an Edinburgh hotel lobby on the Sunday morning after Murrayfield between two Englishmen, one sporting a braw keeker: 'Nigel, what on earth happened to you?'

'I was in a pub in the city centre after the match. We were having a perfectly normal discussion about the game when suddenly this Scotsman leaned across and punched me for no apparent reason.'

A RUGBY World Cup 'I Mentioned The War But I Think I Got Away With It' award went to Duncan Paterson, Scotland team manager. Praising the Japanese for their tenacity at Murrayfield, and in particular a tackle by the Japanese centre on Scott Hastings, he said: 'They certainly don't take any prisoners.'

OVERHEARD: 'Thae Samosans have been the highlight o' the World Cup.'

AUSTRALIAN women rugby fans are noted for the directness of their approach and explicitness of their language. During a British Lions Australian tour when a player (who shall remain nameless) was approached by a local maiden whose convent education and the finishing school in Switzerland had obviously not worked.

'You're a big lad,' she said to the player, 'How big are you?'

76

'I'm about six foot six when I'm standing up straight,' he replied.

Gazing below his belt, the shameless sheila asked a supplementary question: 'And are you in proportion?' 'Oh no,' the player replied. 'If I was in proportion I'd be nine foot eight.'

SPOTTED scrawled on one of the many pillars supporting Glasgow's Kingston Bridge: 'English Go Home.' And on the next pillar: 'Yes, with the Calcultta Cup. 25–7.'

A LOCAL restaurant was negotiating to put some sponsorship into Irvine RFC. The snag was that the restaurateur wanted the name of his establishment to be incorporated into the name of the club. The Irvine committee had to decline on the grounds that they could not see the SRU being too pleased with such scorelines as: Watsonians 6, The Gulab Tandoori Irvine RFC 11.

ISLAY rugby club played hosts to a David Sole select XV. The Diary reported that as well as enjoying the game, Sole and co. also had a grand time at the post-match ceilidh. Freddie Bell, president of the Islay club, was intrigued subsequently to receive a phone call from a lady on the staff of the *Sunday Sport*. She wanted the full story of the goings-on at the ceilidh. It was very enjoyable but nothing unusual for Islay, he replied. Come, come, insisted the lady reporter. What about these international players taking their clothes off at the ceilidh?

Freddie confessed to not having a clue what she was talking about. 'You know what I mean,' she persisted. 'This strip the willow . . .'

AT a time when the community of Monklands district was riven with discord it was heartening to see the Corinthian sport of rugby going some way to ameliorate Lanarkshire's version of the Serbo-Croat way of life. The Waysiders club of Airdrie and Drumpellier from Coatbridge agreed to merge. After a poor season which saw both clubs relegated from their respective divisions in the McEwan's National League, a decision was made to have one rugby club represent the Twin Burghs of the Plain.

The union was achieved not without rancour, especially from Waysiders who had to forsake their clubhouse and make their way to the other side of the Monklands faultline for a pint and a game of rugby. The most memorable contribution to the merger debate came from a player who expressed his reservations in a typically North Lanarkshire down-to-earth manner: 'They're a load o' shite. We're a load o' shite. And if we amalgamate we'll have an even bigger load o' shite.'

ONE of the Diary's more esoteric interests is unusual line-out codes used by rugby teams. An observer at Westerlands playing fields at Anniesland was able to compare the secret codes of Glasgow University and their opponents Strathclyde Police. The yooni chaps stuck to mundane numbers such as 'Seven, Six, Three, Five!'. The polis, you may not be surprised to hear, preferred such instructions as 'Foxtrot, Alpha, Tango, Romeo'.

ENGLAND won the war of words as well as the World Cup Sevens rugby at Murrayfield. While our fans were indulging in some booing and jeering of the English, one of the fans from down south came away with a moment of genuine humour. As Japan scored their 26th point against Scotland in the final of the Bowl, the cup for the runners-up to the runners-up, the Englishman turned to sundry nearby Scots and said in an impeccable Bill McLaren: 'Aye, they'll be smiling down in Tokyo tonight . . .'

FOOTBALL

ONE of the tribulations of the summer of 1991 for Scottish football fans was having to put up with the 25th anniversary of that match at Wembley when those brave West German lads were cheated of the World Cup. Like the party of Scots from East Kilbride who had to cope with some of those typically lovable Cockney types in a Spanish holiday resort. 'Oi, Jock,' said one of the Cockneys, brandishing an English tabloid newspaper, 'Ere's a competition wot you lot should go for. The prize is a day wiv the men who won the World Cup for England.' 'Nae fear,' a Scot replied. 'Who wants to spend a day wi' a Russian referee and linesman?'

THE honeymoon period was short for Tony Cascarino, the £1.1m Celtic forward who suffered a long drought before scoring in a competitive match for the club. The Jokeline was soon buzzing:

- What is the difference between Tony Cascarino and Boris Becker? Boris Becker hits the net sometimes.
- What was the first question Terry Waite asked after his release in Beirut? Has Cascarino scored for Celtic yet?'
- *Follow, Follow*, the Rangers fanzine, described Tony Cascarino as 'the biggest waste of money since Madonna's dad bought her a pair of pyjamas.'

FROM Liverpool we had a variation on the 'Watch your car for you, mister?' urchin school of marketing. In this case the driver, reluctant to fork out the £1, pointed to the Rottweiler in the back of the car. 'Look,' said the urchin to his accomplice, 'this guy's got a Rottweiler that can put out fires.'

A LITTLE-KNOWN fact about the Gulf War was that Saddam Hussein launched a Scud missile at Glasgow. It hit Celtic Park and caused £3m worth of improvements.

YOU have to admire the dedication of your average football mandarin. Take David Will, chairman of Brechin City and a vice-president of Fifa, the sport's ruling body. There he was with Mrs Will at the World Cup draw in New York in 1991, doggedly making his way round a succession of dinners and official receptions. And him just back from a Fifa trip to China. It's amazing how the Angus lawyer manages to fit all this in as well as guiding Brechin City to their dominating position in the lower half of the Scottish second division. One thing he doesn't have to worry about in his Fifa travels is choosing what to wear. He was spotted in the Big Apple sporting a very smart grey suit with a small and stylish Fifa logo. Likewise his shirt and tie. We cannot say if Fifa also provide underpants.

IT can be embarrassing for a young man when he has to make excuses to his contemporaries for not being able to turn up for the Saturday football match. Such a chap was Big Ian who is now a Glasgow GP and as a youth was a Greenock Morton supporter. One Saturday, he had to explain to his chums that he had recently taken up with a young lady and had to attend a course for Good Catholic Engaged Couples. The course contained advice on activities in which the aforementioned Good Catholic Engaged Couples could participate without risk of any untoward naughtiness. Scanning the list, Big Ian alighted on the sport of beagling. We have no information as to how proficient Big Ian and his lady became at following the beagles. Our informant told us that to this day, his peers still greet him with: 'Off beagling again tonight, Ian?'

A NEWLY wed Aberdeen fan's dear wife was wont to throw tantrums and insist he miss the game and accompany her on Saturday-afternoon shopping expeditions. His chums advised him to take a firm stand. The next time she tried to prevent his attendance at Pittodrie he was to put her over his knee and give her a good skelping. Thus there was the scene where this new household was rent with cries of discord. Enraged at her intransigence, the husband chased the wife into the bedroom, put her over his knee and spanked her. It was at this point that the thought occurred to him that the Dons weren't playing all that well at the time.

HAVE you heard about the Irish indoor football competition where they had to have a pitch inspection? The event was the Guinness Sixes held at the Dundonald Ice Bowl, Belfast. The ice rink is often used for non-slippery events by the simple expedient of laying a thick carpet over

the ice. This was duly done for the Guinness Sixes, and a green footballing surface placed on top. Fine and dandy it was too until some bright spark turned off the compressor which was keeping the ice solid. The ice melted and the indoor pitch was soon waterlogged. The organisers were left in a quandary: if they put the compressor back on, the ice would freeze and the Irish would make the Guinness Book of Records for the first indoor soccer tournament cancelled because of a frozen pitch. They persevered with the squeegee mops and got most of the water off the pitch. Viewers of BBC Northern Ireland were treated, however, to the sight of players at the sixes plunging through pools of water.

WHEN Motherwell FC won the Tennent's Scottish Cup final, an immediate reaction was: 'This means they'll be in Europe – just like their local councillors.'

AS a young Rangers player, Alex Ferguson, now manager of Manchester United, was unhappy at being left out of the first team. He stormed into the office of legendary manager Scott Symon. 'Why have I been in the second team for three weeks?' he asked. The magisterial Mr Symon replied: 'Because we don't have a third team.'

BOBBY Lennox, who played with Celtic during the good old Jock Stein, nine-in-a-row years, still plays the odd game in a team which consists of former players and media personalities. During a post-match, fluid-replacement and winding-down session, Mr Lennox lost a wager and as a forfeit had to sing *The Sash*. He got as far as: 'It is old and it is beautiful/And its colours they are fine . . .' Then he stopped. Asked to sing the rest, Mr Lenox confessed that he did not know any more of the words. He explained: 'When I was playing for Celtic, the Rangers fans would start to sing *The Sash*. But by the time they got to the second line we had usually scored and shut them up.'

NINTENDO have come up with Goals – an entertainment which for a mere £40 allows you 'to participate in an actual simulation of the World Cup'. The computer game was obviously created with the American market in mind. The blurb enthuses with considerable Corinthian spirit: 'Win amateur soccer's most glorious prize: the World Cup.' It goes on to explain how you can guide one of 16 national teams to a 'one- game' final. The final includes Japan but not Scotland. The Nintendo chaps obviously knew more than Andy Roxburgh about Scotland's chances.

Under hints on tactics, the instruction manual defines tackling as 'hooksliding' and adds: 'A safe strategy is shooting the ball as far upfield as possible . . . it's a more effective strategy than trying slowly to move the ball upfield by dribbling and passing.' Which is, of course, Nin-

tendospeak for 'Get the ba' up the park!'

ABERDEEN FC's young footballers were chosen as guinea pigs for a Scottish Professional Footballers' Association coaching course on how to deal with the media. 'Young players often have to face the media and many are not properly equipped to portray the proper image of themselves and the club,' said the course organiser. 'Our aim is to teach them what to do and what not to do to present the public with a good image.' Unfortunately the course clashed with a decision by the then Aberdeen manager Alex Smith, who was upset by speculation that his jaiket was on a shaky nail, to issue an edict banning individual players from talking to the media.

IF you have ever wondered what football physios have in those huge bags which they lug on to the park to treat injured players, goalkeeper Gordon Marshall provided a wee insight. When he was with Falkirk, manager Jim Duffy, doubling as physiotherapist, came on to the park and discovered he had nothing in his bag but a sponge and some hair gel. Ever the quick thinker, Jim simply ran some gel through the player's hair and told him: 'You look great. Now get up and play!'

WE know the English broadcasters occasionally have trouble with the names of Scottish football teams. But we fear the chap on BBC Radio Lancashire went too far when he announced as a score draw an encounter between Alloa and Stenhousemanure.

CONTRARY to some opinion, Ernie Walker, the former secretary of the Scottish Football Association, did not spend all his time travelling the world on SFA and FIFA business. Mr Walker apparently makes a regular point of taking in a football match from the fan's point of view. Thus, he was to be found in Annan to attend a Scottish Cup match between the local Athletic and Queen's Park. 'How much is it?' Ernie asked the man at the turnstile. 'Two pounds,' was the reply and, as Mr Walker reached for his wallet, 'but it won't be two pounds to you.' Just as Ernie was about to insist that, even though he was SFA secretary he would pay to get in, the turnstile man added: 'It's only a pound for pensioners.'

SCOTTISH football fans overheard in a bar–restaurant in Cyprus: 'I'm getting worried about the Big Man up there dancing wi' that bloke,' said one of his friends. 'It's OK,' another said, 'it's common for men to dance with each other over here.' 'I know,' the first replied. 'But that's six dances he's had wi' him and two of them were slow numbers.'

Also: 'Do you know why Cypriots are so bad at football? Every time they get a corner they open a fruit shop.'

LEGEND has it that Lou Macari did not become manager of Celtic in 1991 because of his frankness at the interview. What would he do if he were manager, the board members asked. 'I'd sell Paul McStay for £3m and John Collins for £2m,' said Macari. The board, rather cheered at the thought of this substantial cash injection for the Biscuit Tin, asked: 'And then what would you do?' 'Simple,' replied Macari, 'put the lot on Rangers to win the Premier League.'

IT may be hard to believe now but when Mark Hateley first joined Rangers he was the subject of some booing and jeering because he had taken Ally McCoist's place. There was a swift change in heart, perhaps to do with him scoring loads of goals. The jeers were replaced with the refrain: 'Have we told you, Hateley, that we love you . . .'

WHEN Graeme Souness was still an Ibrox hero, the fans regularly chanted 'Sou-ness, Sou-ness'. At one match a press photographer's messenger, who could best be described as being on the chunky side, walked along the trackside to collect some film. As he did so, a section of the fans changed their chant to 'Sumo, sumo . . .'

IN the days when Stirling Albion played on an Astroturf surface, a Kilmarnock player sustained a bad cut. As he lay receiving attention on the Annfield artificial pitch, a Stirling Terracing Tam shouted out: 'Hey, ref. Get him aff. He's bleeding on our carpet.'

THE scene is a campsite in Asti, Italy, during World Cup 1990. Two Scottish fans by the names of Joe and Sugsy, complete with ankle-length kilts, are impressing fellow campers of all nationalities with their culinary skills. They have decided to dine on bacon and beans. They return from the supermarket complaining loudly about the price of streaky bacon in Italy – about £12 a half-pound. Not only is it expensive but ye jist cannae fry it right, opines Sugsy before throwing the lot away. A terrible waste of good Parma ham, say campers who are a touch better informed about Italian nosh.

When the time comes to leave the Italian campsite, Franco the host gives a farewell party to the fans and makes pizzas to order. When Joe is asked what pizza topping he wants, it transpires his taste buds do not extend to tomato, cheese, or any of the other fancy Italian bits. 'Just butter,' he says.

SPOTTED perambulating the streets of sunny Norrkoping during the European Championships in 1992 was none other than Ernie Walker, a former secretary of the Scottish Football Association. Ernie was recognised by a passing Scots fan and asked: 'How's aboot a photie?' Ernie agreed and the fan engaged the services of a passing Dutch fan. The Dutchman duly took the snap and said: 'Now it is my turn.' As Ernie prepared to have his picture taken again, he was handed the camera by the Dutchman who put his arm around the Scots fan.

THE Scottish football fans won the hearts and minds of the Swedish during the championships by taking a wee drink but causing no trouble, while the English continued to disgrace the good name of Britain. One of the Tartan army in Gothenburg reported seeing a Scot, the worse for drink, being looked after by a Swede: 'It's the first time I've ever seen a drunk being carried into a bar by a bouncer.'

BUT the visits to Wembley to play the Auld Enemy used to bring out the worst in Scottish fans. Like the detachment who were billeted in a hotel just outside London. The bears were preparing themselves for the night out ahead by relaxing at their windows and balconies. Among the strollers below were a group of Scots carrying rucksacks. After an exchange of pleasantries between the balcony hangers and the street people, one of the latter, not relishing another night under the stars and loth to waste good drinking money on a hotel, asked: 'Hiv ye a spare bed up there? Ah've naewhere tae sleep.' 'Hang on and I'll see,' was the reply. A couple of minutes later the voice floated down from above: 'Nae bother, pal. Here you go.' Closely followed by a nice wee single bed with sheets and matching pillow.

THIS story is from a Glasgow fan who wishes to remain anonymous in case his wheelchair pass for future international matches is withdrawn. The SFA had been most helpful in arranging special disabled tickets for the Italia 90 World Cup. A kind lady at Park Gardens sent him a letter which he had to produce at Genoa tourist office to collect the tickets. Unfortunately, he had to cancel at the very last minute. He tried to let the SFA know but the officials had already left for Italy. It being a shame to waste the valuable tickets, the letter was passed on to another Scots fan. Thus a fan turned up, in a wheelchair hired from a local hospital, to collect the tickets. He was somewhat taken aback to find the mayor of Genoa there in person to present him with VIP tickets for the match. As our informant said: 'It was, perhaps, just as well that Scotland's performance against Costa Rica did not induce such a state of euphoria as to inspire the seated fan to leap to his feet.'

EVEN lady Scottish football fans have been known to stray. The scene is Barcelona in 1972 where Rangers' European Cup-Winner's Cup glory is being somewhat marred by a post-match riot. It is five a.m. and a group of Rangers fans are returning to Calella, swapping horror stories about the fate suffered by Rangers fans. One occupant says that he is worried about his wife. 'The last time I saw her she was wrestling with a Guardia Civil in the centre circle. If she's in the pokey, I'm in stook because the travellers' cheques are in her name.'

THE best-selling video in the souvenir shop at Parkhead for the last four years? *Celtic, the Road to the Tennents Sixes.*

WE'RE not saying Airdrieonians are strangers to European competition but when they qualified in 1992, the staff at UEFA in Geneva could be heard referring to a team called Airdrie-Onions.

ST Mirren fans have always had a way with words. One denizen of Love Street, concerned that his team were not taking the direct route to goal, was heard to observe: 'They're jist goin' roon' an' roon' in squares.'

AN exhibition at the People's Palace in Glasgow dealing with 500 years of the Roman Catholic Church in the West of Scotland mentioned, of course, the contribution to the community of Celtic FC. It told how in 1888 Brother Walfrid and sundry other Catholic men of good standing formed a football club with the object of raising cash to feed the hungry and clothe the poor of the mainly Irish immigrant population of the East End of Glasgow. The exhibition featured a photograph of an early Celtic team. Except that subsequent research showed the photograph had been wrongly captioned in the museum files. It wasn't Celtic but another Glasgow football team. The captain's badge, a lion rampant, might have given a clue. Yes, it was none other than Rangers.

AFTER a lengthy goal famine had struck Scotland, it was rumoured that on one foreign trip, striker Gordon Durie couldn't find his way into the team hotel. Someone had painted goalposts over the door.

STUART Slater, Celtic's talented, goal-shy £1.5m purchase from West Ham, became known to fans as Jigsaw. Why? Because he falls apart when he gets into the box.

CELTIC'S failure to attract a sponsor led to some ribaldry. For a team who had not won a trophy for four years, Winalot seemed an obvious choice. Then it was said that Oxo were interested. They planned to launch a special Celtic cube, in green, white and gold foil, to be known as the Laughing Stock.

It was reported that Celtic had at last found a sponsor for their new £50m stadium at Cambuslang. The Tooth Fairy.

ITALIAN football just oozes style. Even down to the objects thrown by the crowd. Colin Davidson, a producer with *Scotsport Extra Time*, who found himself with a film crew behind the goals at an AC Milan home game, narrowly missed being crowned by a flying bottle of salad cream.

AT least someone has a sense of humour at Celtic Park. After the most barren and unsuccessful spell in the club's recent history, Celtic Pools ran a competition for supporters to say in no more than 12 words 'why Celtic are the best team in Europe'. Despite repeated requests, the Diary was never able to find out from Celtic what was the winning answer.

THERE appears to be no bounds to the allergy your average Celtic has to anything remotely connected with Rangers. We hear of one Tim on a construction site who hated using the platform lift because it had made a company called Alimac. This meant it was an Alimac hoist.

WHEN Celtic introduced their own brand of peanuts, there was a promotional offer of a free packet for every fan who spent £1.50 or more at the Parkhead refreshment stalls. Thus we heard from a member of the Celtic Park faithful who, having purchased his two pies, two Bovrils, crisps, and Mars bar, walked away to these words from the girl behind the counter: 'Haw, are ye no wantin' your nuts?'

WHILE most Celtic fans were swallowing the bitter pill and uttering phrases of congratulation as Rangers came close to winning a European Cup final place, it was not given to every Tim to be so sporting. Like the chap was heard to say: 'If that happens, the best we can hope for is a plane crash.'

TERRY Cassidy achieved some notoriety in his brief but abrasive period as Celtic's chief executive. He even achieved the accolade of sharing a joke with Saddam Hussein. Saddam visits the mosque and asks Allah: 'Tell me, Allah, am I the baddest, worstest man on earth or what?' Allah refers him to the magic mirror, of which he asks: 'Mirror, mirror, on the wall, who is the baddest of them all?' He gets his answer but is somewhat puzzled. Back he goes to Allah with the supplementary question: 'Who is this guy Terry Cassidy?'

ONE of Terry Cassidy's innovations at Parkhead was to hire a team of crack marketing men. One of these chaps was given the task of creating a new Celtic FC tie. Various designs were put forward to Mr Cassidy, followed by the question: 'What colour did you have in mind?' The boss, in a burst of uncharacteristic diplomacy, replied: 'I think we'll stick with green.'

IT was rumoured that the reason for Mr Cassidy's eventual sacking was that, when asked by the Celtic board how to save money on the new stadium, he replied: 'Don't build a trophy room.'

SHORTLY after the change of management at Ibrox in 1991, Ally McCoist revealed that he would have to undergo an operation before he could resume full duties for club and country. It was nothing to do with ankles or hamstrings. The Greatest Living Ranger said he was to be hospitalised for an operation 'to remove this smile I've had on my face ever since Souness left'.

THIS tale of a footballing odyssey to Marseille concerns a Lanarkshire lawyer who had been persuaded by his pals that nothing would do but they would all take themselves off on the day-return flight to take in the Rangers European Cup match. He agreed to go but decided to keep it a secret from she who must be obeyed. Mainly because she wouldn't have let him go.

Thus he left the matrimonial home dressed as if he was off to the office. Yes, he was the guy on the Marseille charter wearing the pin-stripe suit. He proceeded to have a jolly time until, as ill luck would have it, he was separated from his chums and found himself at the game in the midst of the dreaded Marseille fans. Worse still, he found himself being jostled and, fearing that he was the victim of a gang of Marseille cutpurses, he did what any Lanarkshire man would do, he resorted to physical force. Unfortunately they were not French felons but ordinary fans that he was assaulting and our man ended up in custody.

When he was eventually released at 11.30 p.m., his plane to Glasgow was long gone. You can imagine the trepidation with which he made the phone call: 'Hello, dear, I'm in Marseille . . .' Our man was last seen carrying home an Easter egg as big as himself.

THE PUG

TO most people, pugs are ugly little brutes with flattened faces cruelly disfigured by years of inbreeding. To their owners, they are paragons of beauty and bursting with character.

The main trouble with pugs is that they are addictive. An American author described the pug as 'the perfect blend of little-dog appeal and wistfulness and big-dog stamina and courage'. The Duchess of Windsor had a troupe of 11 of the beasts which was probably excessive. But one is definitely not enough.

Another problem with pugs is that they are not cheap to buy off the peg. Our first, Sophie, cost £200. So we decided to venture into the unknown territory of DIY. With a little help, of course, from Sophie.

We had been warned by Sophie's breeder, a formidable lady from East Lothian whose dogs have had many successes at Crufts, that pugs 'are not very sexy'. It was a great relief to leave the technical details of the mating to her. She selected one of her own dogs, Benjamin, as Sophie's suitor.

Readers of a delicate disposition may prefer to skip the next few paragraphs detailing the creation process.

It involved some dexterity on the part of the human go-between, a lot of patience, and a Mars bar. For a wee dog who was supposed not to be sexy, Benjy certainly seemed interested as the proceedings got under way. Our Sophie seemed merely confused.

First the male was helped into position and turned 180 degrees clockwise. The breeder then held both the pugs' tails in one hand and waited for 20 minutes.

Then, with a cry of 'Mars bar for Benjy!' it was all over. Benjy's sweet reward explained his enthusiasm.

Sophie's reward was to come nine weeks later. She went into labour, with impeccable timing, just as the family were about to leave for a wedding.

She was to prove less than competent as a mother and didn't seem to have a clue what was happening. The humans weren't much better off, despite mugging up beforehand with various textbooks. The first puppy was dead on arrival. None of the recommended courses of action, from rubbing vigorously with a towel to clasping it in both hands and waving it up and down, had prevailed.

The second and last pup appeared 20 minutes later – feet first. At least

the feet were kicking. Somehow, the unwilling mother managed to deliver the surviving member of her litter to accompanying cries of 'PUSH! PUSH!' from the chief midwife.

The nightmare had only just begun. The less-than-radiant mother would have nothing to do with her offspring. When she wasn't trying to shove it out of the box, she ignored it.

The puppy, after a cursory examination, was named Florence. She was wrapped in doggy swaddling clothes and left on top of a hot-water bottle for warmth while the vet was summoned.

The vet, it must be said, was less than encouraging. He told us he didn't rate the pup's chances of survival at more than 50 per cent, given

the attitude of the mother. He inspected the corpse of the dead pup, gave the mother an injection, produced a portable bill dispenser, took his cheque for £28 and left. It was never like this in the James Heriot books.

For the next five days, Florence the pup had to be force-fed. To be exact, the recalcitrant mother, Sophie, had to be held down while Florence was attached for feeding.

These were difficult times, especially for the chief midwife who supervised most of the feeds. But the good news was that Florence was putting on weight and seemed likely to confound the vet's prognosis.

Five days later, Florence was taken to the vet for her first check-up. She

90

Asda is a smoke free zone

Guide dogs excepted

passed with flying colours except for one small detail. Florence was a boy. In the heat of the moment, and possibly in the chief midwife's desire to have a second bitch pug, Florence's maleness had been overlooked. As the vet pointed out, the presence of nipples and the absence of testicles in a day-old pup are not reliable indicators.

But the main thing was that Patrick (né Florence) was a survivor. Even when his wicked mother refused to be held down while he fed, he took kindly to receiving his nourishment from a spoon.

As he grew, his mother showed no signs of developing maternal instincts. If anything she developed feral instincts towards Patrick. Sophie would casually leave a dog biscuit to tempt Patrick. When he began to eat it, she would pounce on him with a swiftness and ferocity which earned her the nickname of The Cobra.

Patrick has survived many vicissitudes in his first six months. He suf-

fered an adverse reaction to his Parvo-Virus injection and his already malformed face swelled to bulldog-like proportions. He almost scratched his own eye out. He had developed bow legs from over-exercise.

At the age of six months the good news was that his mother had started showing an interest in him. The bad news was that she was in heat and was trying to seduce him. Apart from telephoning Esther Rantzen's child abuse helpline, there was little we could do except try to keep the pre-incestuous couple apart. He even seems to have survived this psychological onslaught.

When the time comes for the complement of pugs at Chateau Shields to be increased, it will be Patrick who will be thrown into the breeding arena. Twenty minutes of tension at the beginning seems to be a better deal than weeks of misery at the other end.

Pugs who wish to share a Mars bar with Patrick should apply in writing, enclosing full pedigree details.

APOCRYPHAL TALES

WE heard of one Glasgow infant who appeared to enjoy his holidays in the South of France. His mother was making a belated attempt to wean the toddler off the breast. As we said, the wee lad had a great time. His mother didn't really. Spending, as she did, much time prising her hungry son off a number of very surprised women on the topless beach.

NOT only were souls saved during Billy Graham's last evangelistic mission to Scotland, but wee faith-healing miracles were also being done. Thus it was that two poor unfortunates, a woman on crutches and a man with a terrible stutter, went forward to be cured. They both went behind a screen on the stage while the great man led the prayers on their behalf. 'Senga, throw away your left crutch,' he cried. The left crutch came flying over the screen. 'Senga, throw away your right crutch,' he cried. The right crutch came flying over the screen. There was a loud thump. Billy shouted out: 'Shuggie, what has happened?'

'S-s-s-she's f-f-f-f-fell o-o-o-on h-h-h-h-her a-a-a-a-arse,' came the reply.

THE Diary pursued this story to the ends of the earth – well, Banffshire, actually where it was supposed to have happened. It starts with an advertisement in the cars-for-sale column of a Banffshire local newspaper. The ad says 'BMW for sale. £10'. Everyone assumes it is a misprint. But one chap phones up to find out what the price should be. 'No. £10 is the correct price,' says the lady at the other end of the phone. 'But a BMW of that age and model is worth at least £7,000,' the chap replies. The lady, in a firm tone of voice, says the price is £10. The deal is duly done. The explanation is that the car belonged to the lady's husband. The same husband who had left for South Africa with the new woman in his life. 'What about the BMW?' his wife had asked as he left. 'Oh, just sell it and send me on the proceeds,' he said.

THIS story is set in one of the swish glass lifts of the terribly upmarket Princes Square shopping centre in Glasgow. Among the passengers are a woman and her wee boy, aged about seven. The wee boy is proudly sporting a new pair of those trainers that cost the best part of £100. Also in the lift is an attractive woman who, during the journey, turns round and slaps the man standing beside her. She says something to the effect that he is a filthy pervert and ought to be arrested. The argument continues after the lift arrives at the ground floor with the angry lady trying to find a security guard. The mother hustles her son away from the scene with words along the lines of, 'Is that not terrible?' Her son agrees and explains: 'She was standing on my new trainers, so I nipped her bum to get her to move.'

A YOUNG lady turns up for an operation at the gynaecology ward. Her hair is dyed green. Her pubic hair is also dyed green. In addition she has a tattoo on her stomach which reads: 'Keep off the grass.' When she comes out of the anaesthetic the nurse tells

her: 'I'm sorry. We had to mow your lawn.'

A TALE from Greenock of yesteryear concerns a local businessman who at the age of 70 married his young secretary. The local paper reported: 'The groom's gift to the bride was an antique pendant.'

A LANARKSHIRE youth football team went to Paris to take part in a tournament. Everything was going very smoothly for the team. They had won both their games. But the team coach was concerned to see that one of his boys, who had been engaged in conversation by some local lads, appeared to be on the verge of a spot of fisticuffs. The coach intervened and asked the lad, who was from Larkhill, what the problem was. 'He swore at me,' said the Lanarkshire boy. The French boys, rather taken aback at his reaction, explained that they had merely asked if the Scottish team had been the winner, or *vainqueur*, of their section.

THE Diary was inundated with versions of this apocryphal story. We heard variously of the lawyer from Dundee, the old lady from Dunfermline, and the Glasgow policeman who was in a lift in a New York hotel. Also in the lift was a well-heeled black chap and his minder. 'Hit the floor,' barked the well-heeled chap. The Scottish lawyer/old lady/policeman promptly dived to the floor, only to hear the laughter of the other two occupants as the minder pressed a button on the lift control panel. The story ends when the lawyer/old lady/policeman goes to pay the bill and finds it has already been taken care of by the rich chap in the lift – film star Eddie Murphy, who says he has not laughed so much since the last time he was at the bank.

THIS from a friend of a prison warden in one of the country's young offenders' institutions. There's a young lady who comes to the institution every Sunday morning to give Bible classes to the captive audience. On one visit she returned to her car to discover she had locked her keys inside the vehicle. She asked if she could phone her husband who would come out with the spare set. The warden replied that there were plenty of people around who could get into her car no bother. He proceeded to ask which inmates were in 'for doing cars'. A youth volunteered, and was taken out to the car and asked to use his skills to gain entry thereto. The youth appeared rather bemused, but obliged by launching a brick through the windscreen.

ON a coach transporting holidaymakers from Glasgow to Paris, many of them on their way to sample Euro Disney, what does the courier person spot but a little old lady sitting with a TV set on her lap. 'Why are you taking a TV set to Paris?' is the obvious question. 'I don't want to miss *Coronation Street*,' is the reply. 'But

French television doesn't have *Coronation Street*.' 'Exactly. That's why I'm taking my own set.'

THE scene is a busy intersection in the centre of Glasgow. A pensioner from Bearsden is sitting at the lights in his beloved Ford Sierra (one careful owner). He is driving home after a sally into the dirty, dangerous traffic of Glasgow, having dropped his daughter off at Queen Street station. Suddenly a policeman jumps into the back seat and shouts the fabled words: 'Follow that car.' The auld fella is a bit disconcerted but says he will do his best. 'On you go then,' says the polisman.
'But the lights are at red,' the driver replies.
'On you go,' the copper insists.
'Very well, then,' says the driver. He adjusts his mirror. He straightens his bunnet. He notices that one of his driving gloves (the kind with the holes punched in the leather) has become unbuttoned. He buttons it. Now he is ready to go in hot pursuit of the stolen car. (By this time the lights had changed to green.)
'Mirror, signal, pull out,' the old chap is saying to himself as he sets off. What the polis, head in hands, is saying in the back seat is not printable except that he indicated there was no point in continuing the car chase.

THIS is a true story about an oil-rig worker who suffered from a terrible sore throat whenever he was working offshore. He awoke each morning with a nasty taste in his mouth. He had an irritating cough which lasted all day long. Naturally he was worried about this, and each time he went on leave he would get himself along to the doctor. But the doctor could never find anything wrong.

The chap was begining to fear the worst. Back on the rig, the sore throat came back. He confided his fears to his workmates as they sat at their tea. At this point the workmate with whom he shared a room said that it was time he came clean. The sore throats were probably his fault. Why, the ailing chap asked.

'Well, you're an almighty snorer,' his pal replied. 'I can't get to sleep for the noise. So, one night when you were lying on your back, mouth open, I dropped some soap powder down your throat. It stopped the snoring so I've been using it ever since.'

FOR this tale we have to go back to a green, grassy slope adjacent to the River Boyne late in the evening of 12 July 1690. King Billy, for it is he, is wandering around the battlefield. He chances upon his father-in-law, the vanquished King James VII as was, sitting dejectedly on the aforemen-

tioned green, grassy slope.

'I can't believe it,' King James says to King Billy. 'I don't know how we managed to lose. We outnumbered you. We out-manoeuvred you. We outflanked you . . .'

'Don't worry about it,' King Billy reassures him. 'It's just another battle. In a fortnight's time who'll remember the Battle of the Boyne?'

A JAPANESE soldier emerges from the Malaysian jungle many years after the end of the Second World War. He is duly flown home to be reunited with his wife. After an emotional reunion, with much ritual bowing, the husband asks his wife: 'Honourable wife, have you been faithful to me?'

To which she replies: 'Honourable husband, I have indeed been faithful.' The husband continues: 'Honourable wife, I think you lie. I have heard you've been living with a Gordon Highlander from Inverurie.'

'Fa tellt ye that?' she demands.

THIS apparently true tale comes from a member of the ground staff at Kennedy Airport, New York, where a wifie from Glasgow arrived, carrying her pet budgie in a cage. On her arrival, the customs officers promptly confiscated the budgie, whereupon she burst into tears. As the wifie contemplated a budgieless existence she pleaded to the aforementioned ground hostess: 'Can ye no' see by his wee face that he's breaking his heart?'

This, however, was not strictly true. Throughout the official investigations, the budgie was chirping loudly: 'I'm in America! I'm in America!' as he had been learnt by the old lady especially for the occasion. The budgie was eventually allowed to pass unhindered into the land of the free and the home of the brave.

A GIRL was sobbing in the maternity ward and the doctor asked the sister why. 'She can't breast feed,' answered sister. 'Then you know what to do,' he went on. 'It's hardening of the nipples. Get some olive oil and cotton wool and make up some soaks and get her to put them on.' Upon his departure the sister consoled the girl: 'It's all right, dear. Doctor wants you to put on some olive-oil soaks.'

'Awright,' said the lassie. 'I'll put them oan if ye want – but will they no make a hell o' a mess of ma feet?'

A TALE about confusion in Highland dancing circles. A teacher from deepest Argyll offered his assistance to the organiser of a Highland dancing competition in darkest Govan. He was allocated the job of checking off the names and numbers of the competitors. All went well until he was approached and addressed by a young lady. He scanned his list of competitors and had to admit: 'I'm sorry, I don't seem to have a Joanna Pye down here. Which section are you dancing in, dear?'

'Ah'm no' in any section,' she replied. 'Ah'm fae the kitchen. D'ye wanna pie?'

A TALE from Kilbirnie which indicates that the spirit of integration is alive and well in that north Ayrshire fastness. A local woman is walking past the statue outside the Walker Hall when she spots a young Chinese boy, second son of the local restaurateur, clambering to the top of the 12ft statue. She remonstrates with the boy, telling him that he is in danger of falling and breaking his neck. The Kilbirnie wifie concludes her wee speech with the information that she is 'gaun tae tell his faither'. The Chinese Kilbirnie boy replies: 'Hah! You don't know who ma faither is!'

A NEWLY hired travelling salesman wrote his first sales report to the office. Its sheer illiteracy stunned the top brass: 'I have seen this lot what hasn't never bot nuthin fromm us, and I sole them a buncha goods for a thousand quid. I am now going to Manncester.'

Before he could be given the sack, or at least sent on a course for to learn English, there came this letter from Manchester: 'I cum hear an sole them haff a millyun.'

The next morning the two letters were tacked to the staff bulletin board with this memo from the managing director: 'We bin spending two much time trying to spel insted of sel. You should all gett out an do wot he dun.'

THE scene is a Glasgow park on the day of the big Orange walk. A chap heavily laden with a suitcase approaches a polisman and asks if it would be in order for him to set up a small bookstall. The policeman can think of no objections but asks the chap what books he would be selling. It is a book on King William, the very hero of the Orange Order types who have taken over the park for the purpose of celebrating the Battle of the Boyne.

That will be of great interest to the lieges, the PC observes. 'Yes,' says the author and publisher. 'It's the true story of King William. Did you know he didn't have a white horse and he was a homosexual . . .?' On police advice, the bookstall was not set up.

THE personnel section of a Govan firm organised a series of interviews for junior clerical posts. The personnel officer is none too hopeful, having spent two days wading through application forms which list hobbies such as 'walking my pit-bull' and 'playing darts'. These, incidentally, from the female applicants. 'Wheel the first one in,' ordains the personnel officer.

The hopeful young lady enters the room, keen to make a good impression and tries to be as outgoing and chatty as possible. Pulling at her blouse where sweat is sticking it to her body, she ventures the meteorological comment: 'Soafy clammy!'

'Come in, Miss Clammy. Take a seat,' says the personnel officer.

THIS tale concerns an Italian café owner in a small Scots town who never quite mastered the English language. This made him easy prey for local youths who delighted in taking the mickey. He would be asked at various times, to his confusion and frustration, for a 'packet o' bumbee's feathers' or a 'quarter o' roon squares'. In addition to the verbals, the callow youths were not averse to flinging their hot-pea specials at each other. Then, one Christmas, overdosing on goodwill, the lads decided to stop giving the old man such a hard time.

They called him over to their table and informed him of their intention to reform. His delight was huge. 'Yerraverranicea boays,' he exclaimed. 'Nae maira roona squares or bumbee feathers or scoota peas a' owera ma shoap. Itsa great! An' ah'll dae something forra you boays. Ah'll no spit in yer coaffee nae mair!'

MANY years ago, an Italian café in Perth had a windy-up gramophone which was a target for mischief by the local bad boys. So much so that the café proprietor used to reprimand them with the words: 'Hey, boays. No flicka da peas doon the hoarna the gramophone. You'll choke Harry Lauder.'

SENILITY is not funny. But life is. Thus we pass on to you the story of an old chap sitting crying on a park bench. A kindly young passer-by stops and asks what's the matter. In between heart-rending sobs, the old fellow explains that he recently got married to his next-door neighbour's 22-year-old Swedish au pair. She was a wonderful cook, ironed his shirts beautifully, and kept the house to perfection. She had also rekindled long-forgotten passions. 'So why are you crying?' the kindly passer-by enquired. To which the old chap replied: 'I can't remember where I live.'

THIS story about an announcement by the covener at a soirée at a West of Scotland Labour club has a ring of truth. He stood up, 'twixt the bingo and the band to inform members of the funeral of a stalwart comrade which was taking place on the Monday. The club had hired a double-decker bus and all were urged to attend. 'You know the old saying,' the convener said. 'The more the merrier.'

SHIPYARD humour is not dead: we hear of a Norwegian manager at the Kvaerner yard in Govan who asked a shipwright to walk more quickly to his job, as they do in Norway. Slightly miffed at such a direction, the Clydesider replied: 'Look pal, this is a boiler suit ah'm wearin'! No an effin' track suit!'

A YOUNG student at Glasgow Dental School had been allocated to treat an elderly woman who was being fitted with a new pair of false teeth. On each visit, the woman expressed her gratitude for his care and attention by bringing him a gift of a bag of almonds. The student was always suitably grateful, thanking her very

much and saying how much he liked almonds.

On her last visit, when the wallies had been well installed, the dentist-to-be said to her: 'Thanks for the bags of almonds you've been bringing me; you must have a great supply of them somewhere.' To which she replied: 'Well son, I love thae sugared almonds, but it's just the sugar I like, not the almonds.'

A MOTHER attending a parent/teacher meeting was pleased to hear of her son's progress. His maths had improved greatly and his writing and spelling were excellent. The teacher, however, had been rather disturbed, she explained, to read his latest composition, which had ended with what was described as the 'FU expression'.

The young mother was quite upset and asked what they might do. They decided to seek the help of the principal who, with Solomonic wisdom, decided to have the boy read out his composition to his classmates. This was duly arranged and they listened as the wee boy read his masterpiece. It was the sad tale of a time when he had been looking after a friend's pet rabbit and it had escaped. Many adventures were experienced during the frantic search until he found the absconding bunny under a tree.

'And,' the little boy read aloud, 'I just picked Sammy up, said "phew!" and put him back in his hutch.'

WE heard, via a teacher at a posh

school in Glasgow, that the pupils in such establishments continue to have the highest aspirations despite the economic downturn. A class essay on what the little darlings wanted to be produced a rich crop of brain surgeons, prime ministers, and captains of industry. There was one exception: a boy who, it appeared, wanted to be a carpet layer. The teacher was intrigued. Yes, the boy was not the brightest. Sure, his spelling and handwriting left a lot to be desired. She enquired of the tradesman-to-be: 'Is it a family business? Is your father a carpet layer?'

With a look of disdain the pupil pointed to his words and said: 'Not a carpet layer. A corporate lawyer.'

A MIDWIFE is paying the last of a series of visits to a lady in Bridgeton who's just had another bairn, taking the tribe into double digits.

To mark the occasion, the mother persuades the midwife to stay for a cuppa and a wee scone. The midwife duly compliments the mother on her baking skills, remarking that the scones are delicious. 'Yes,' says the mother, 'I always think they're lighter and tastier when they are made with your own milk.'

TWO elderly women standing in the post-office queue in darkest Hardgate waiting to collect their pensions are showing great interest in a girl in front of them in the queue. She is wearing a pair of 70 denier tights, a form of very thick, very black, and very opaque leggings which are apparently fashionable these days.

As the girl leaves after being served, one old dear turns confidentially to the other and says: 'Mary, do you mind when we were young whit happened to girls who wore thae black woolly stockings?' 'Aye,' Mary replies. 'Nothing.'

A TALE from the Hebrides of a non-fisherman invited for a wee trip on a boat out to gather in the catch from some lobster creels. The guest is feeling queasy because of the slight swell, although a recent dalliance with the drink cannot be ruled out as a factor.

As he is watching the lobster fishermen at work, said chap is overcome and is sick over the side, losing his false teeth in the process. This causes much hilarity among the crew, who decide to prolong the fun.

They borrow the skipper's false teeth and place them in a creel as it is brought on deck. What a miracle, they explain. What a chance in a million for the sea to yield up the dentures which had been so cruelly lost. The victim of their hoax is quite amazed and puts in the said false teeth. But they remain in his mouth for only a few seconds. 'Ach, these aren't my teeth,' he says as he takes out the skipper's dentures and throws them into the sea.

THIS story about a mother and daughter demonstrates the vicissitudes of dealing with an elderly relative who is a few crumbs short of the full Madeira cake. The devoted daughter was out shopping one day when she came across a videotape of her mother's all-time favourite film – *The Bells of St Mary's* starring Bing Crosby. She bought it as a wee treat.

The mother, not at her best that day, was having trouble understanding what a video is. The daughter took the easy way out and told mother simply that her favourite film was on the telly that night.

The pair duly settled down to watch the movie. Towards the end of the film, the daughter realised there was something else on TV that she wanted to see but if they continued to watch *The Bells of St Mary's* she'd miss the start.

She considered but decided against trying to explain to mum that with the wonders of modern technology they could catch the end of the film later. Surreptitiously reaching for the remote control, she fast-forwarded the videotape.

As the film sped by, the old lady spotted something was wrong. 'Is that those people next door hoovering again?' she asked.

GRANNY is looking after her five-year-old grandson who has been sent home in disgrace from school for being cheeky to the jannie. The boy is warned by granny that 'Santa doesn't come to bad boys'.

The boy responds by sticking out his tongue. Time for stern measures. A cuff on the bonce is not politically correct so granny goes into an elaborate number, picks up the telephone, dials a few digits at random, and says: 'Right, Santa, don't bring any presents for . . .' and proceeds to give the wean's name and address. (Which we have withheld, since he may yet appear at the children's panel.)

Granny puts down the phone, quite pleased with her ploy. 'I'll just phone Santa back and tell him it's OK!' responds the uppity bairn. 'You don't know his number,' says granny. After only a few moments thought, the wee man grabs the phone and presses the redial button.

THE Power of Advertising: This tale is from a lady who was busy one day looking after her four-year-old grandson. Said grandson spent most of the time whizzing round her house wearing earphones and pretending he was piloting an aeroplane. Swooping down in front of her he announced that he was about to jump out of his plane. 'Well,' said the granny, 'you will need wings for jumping out of your airplane, won't you?' The wee boy thought for a bit and agreed that he'd probably need Bodyform Plus. His gran was slightly taken aback. Bodyform Plus? 'Yes, Gran,' he said. 'They've got wings you know.'

AN elderly Scots exile lady, over from the States for a holiday, was relating to friends how proud she was of her grandsons. But she was also worried that they were overdoing their volunteer work for the church. She explained that since her arrival they seemed to spend nearly every evening down at the mission and often slept in the next day because of the late hours involved. No one had the heart to tell her that The Mission was the name of a local pub.

THE scene is a safari park which has been blessed by a school trip from the Possil area of Glasgow. A number of the little angels have escaped from their bus and are frolicking in the long grass. A concerned safari park ranger drives up in his *Daktari*-style jeep shouting: 'Boys! The lions! The lions!' To which one of the lads ripostes: 'Don't worry, mister. We never touched your lions.'

A GLASGOW rugby fan is in Paris, in full Highland dress and somewhat the worse for wear having encountered a team of bears from Bordeaux who have forced him to drink much whisky. He has to leave the pub early and retire to his hotel room before he falls down. When his room-mate returns, reasonably sober, he finds the kiltie lying totally naked on the bed apart from his ghillie brogues – those shoes with the criss-cross laces up the leg. Having covered his pal's embarrassment, the room-mate is untying the laces and taking off the brogues when the drunken kiltie comes to. 'Just put my shoes in the wardrobe beside my clothes,' he says.

'What wardrobe?' asks his pal (for it was a very cheap Paris hotel). 'That wardrobe,' says the kiltie, pointing to the verandah door. 'Oh, this wardrobe,' says the room-mate, looking at the full Highland kit lying crumpled in the well of the building four floors below.

A TRUE story, we are told, from a funeral in Glasgow's East End. They are burying old Jimmy, who had been a bit of a drinker till the night he birled home from the pub and died. After his wee lie-in at home (no, it's not the joke about how well Jimmy was looking because he hadn't had a drink for three days) his sons are carrying the coffin out to the hearse. The path is icy and the sons hit a slidy bit. They are weaving left and right in an effort to keep their feet and a hold of the coffin.

The grieving widow, who had never been short of a comment, says: 'Look at that. He's going out the way he always came in.'

CRANHILL, Glasgow, is the scene of this tale of life as it is lived these days. A local minister answers the knock at his manse door to be confronted by a child in the company of an irate parent. The child has a gory head wound, stitches and all. And, says the father, it is all the fault of the church. Kindly explain, says the minister.

Well, explains the father. It's that unbreakable glass in the church windows. His darling child had been engaged in the harmless practice of

goes up to a front door and barks three times. Nothing happens. The dog jumps up and rings the doorbell three times. Eventually the door opens, his owner comes out, takes the shopping bag, and clips the dog round the ear.

Horrified, the onlooker berates the owner for his cruelty to an outstandingly intelligent dog. 'He's clever all right,' says the owner. 'But that's the third time he's lost his front door key.'

MORMONS chapping at your door can be a bore but it is not usual to bring in the polis to deal with them. We heard of a call to a Glasgow police office from a distraught woman claiming that she had been visited by a Mormon. She had slammed the door in his face but he wouldn't go away and was still knocking. When the polis arrived, they discovered that the man was indeed still there and was knocking incessantly. The lady of the house had trapped his coat in the door.

chucking a half-brick at the windows when the aforementioned brick bounced back and hit him on the head.

WE are not sure whether this comes under the heading of Apocryphal Tales or Shaggy Dog Stories but at least it is clean:

A customer in a corner grocer's shop is most impressed to see a dog enter the shop with a shopping bag, wait its turn in the queue, place the bag on the counter, dip inside, find a purse, and give it to the assistant. The grocer takes a shopping list from inside the purse, fills the bag with the requested items, extracts the money, puts the change back into the purse, places the purse inside the bag, and sends the dog off on its way.

The customer, intrigued by this canine talent, decides to follow the dog home. He watches as the dog

A GLASGOW community worker of English ethnic origin had not quite mastered the nuances of the local patois. At a meeting the community worker was desperately trying to get volunteers to form a committee. A wee lady in the front row had her hand half-raised, unsure whether or not to volunteer.

'Ah!' said the English community worker, pointing to the woman.

'What about you?'

'I'm swithering,' the still-undecided woman replies.

'Good,' says the community worker. 'That's Mrs Swithering. Now, anyone else?'

The same community worker announced that she was taking the afternoon off to have a look around the city. 'Are you just going for a wee donner?' asks a colleague of Glasgow ethnic origin. 'Certainly not. I'm a vegetarian,' was the indignant answer.

THIS is a wee tale from the Royal Liff state hospital, Dundee. A refurbishment was in progress and, as part of the material required, a lorryload of sand was delivered. As the driver piloted his lorry through the entrance gates, he was flagged down by a well-dressed chap who enquired what his business was in the hospital.

Having heard the driver's mission, the chap told him to dump the sand at the entrance. Are you sure? the driver asked. Don't argue, do as you're told, the chap replied. The driver duly dumped his load of sand in the driveway, received a signature on his delivery docket, and departed.

Yes, you've guessed. The patient duly walked away leaving the staff to deal with the problem of the pile of sand blocking the driveway.

THIS tale from Dumfries is said to have happened during a recent spell of good weather in the summer of 1993. You remember that bit of good weather. Just before we had the snow. The hero of our story was disporting himself in warm-weather wear and did he not get a wee stone lodged in his sandal. He leaned against a handy metal structure and shook his leg violently in an effort to dislodge the stone. This performance attracted the attention of a passing roadsweeper. And what would you do if you saw a fellow man clutching a power-generator box thing and shaking violently, obviously suffering from an electric shock? You would do exactly what the Dumfries roadsweeper did. Remembering how dangerous electricity is, you would use your brush to whack the man free and save him from electrocution. Even though you might send the bewildered sandal-shaker to hospital in the process for treatment to a broken arm.

NAE LUCK

A BRIDE-TO-BE, after much thought, chose to proceed to the altar to the tune from the film *Robin Hood, Prince of Thieves*. This tune, which you may have heard, is the romantic *Everything I Do, I Do It For You*, by Bryan Adams. The person in charge of the wedding music, being of a different generation, got it slightly wrong. The bride was not impressed to be confronted by the strains of an earlier hit (Gary Miller, circa 1956) with the stirring but decidedly unromantic lyrics: 'Robin Hood, Robin Hood riding through the glen . . .'

PROFESSOR Neil Brooks, a neurosurgery expert at Glasgow University, was booked to give a talk to staff and clients at a day centre in Shettleston on the topic of memory loss and lack of concentration. He failed to turn up because he had forgotten to put the

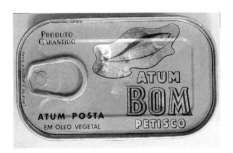

engagement into his diary.

DAVID McNiven, musician of 7:84 and Wildcat fame, told how many years ago he had found a pair of tarnished candlesticks in a bin in Dennistoun. He gave them as a present to a chum. Mr McNiven recently had cause to visit this chum in his new, recently purchased, bijou country retreat. 'It's all thanks to you,' the chum explained. 'Those candlesticks were Charles Rennie Mackintosh and became very valuable. In fact we bought this house with the money they fetched.'

A BUS driver taking a party on a coach tour of the Scottish Borders was invited to join his grateful passengers for high tea. As orders were taken for steak pie, gammon, or chicken, the driver piped up: 'Can I have a cheese salad please, as I do not believe in killing animals for food.' This remark was met by a stony silence. The party he was driving were retired butchers and their wives on an outing organised by the ancient Incorporation of Fleshers of Glasgow.

A NAE Luck Oscar to the Scottish

BRUCE SPRINGSTEIN, 35, has been a proofreader and inventory analyst, processed loan applications and even shagged fuzzy orange basketballs for a car promotion as a temp in Milwaukee, Wisconsin. He has no medical insurance and does not own a car or a house.

Television cameraman who was sent to the Possil housing scheme in Glasgow 'to get background shots for a programme on the drug problem'. The cameraman misheard the instructions. After a day risking life and limb filming in those mean streets, he returned with definitive footage of the alsatians and sundry other dugs who roam the range up Possil way.

107

A SOLDIER in the Royal Scots was out in the desert a few days after the Gulf War ceasefire. There was still the odd alarming bang and thump as shells and other bits of ammunition were disposed of. Our man duly heard a loud bang. Then he noticed a three-legged camel hirple on to the horizon. Poor thing has lost a leg on a land-mine, he thought, before fixing it in his rifle sight and humanely consigning it to the next world. Enter, stage left, an irate Bedouin who had been in pursuit of the camel. The very same camel that was always escaping and one of whose legs he had hobbled up so that it couldn't run away too far.

CHIC MURRAY

A STAGE version of the life story of Chic Murray provided the excuse to bask in the memories of the tall Droll's comic genius. John Bett, who directed the play, was no stranger to going for the occasional dram with Chic. On one occasion they were enjoying a post-theatre thirst-quencher in a seedy London actors' club. Sitting in one of the warren of dungeon-like rooms, they found themselves sharing it with a chap and his Labrador dug. Chic was telling a long story and kept pausing to gaze at the Labrador. The punchline, although Chic Murray never needed punchlines, was: "They've got awfy big rats in here.'

CHIC Murray appeared to have a preoccupation with animals. Strolling through the streets of London, he was stopped and asked: 'Do you know the Battersea Dogs' Home?' To which he replied: 'I didn't even know he'd been away.'

Or his comment: 'Just bought the wife a jaguar. Great investment. It bit her leg off.'

One summer day Chic wandered into a pet shop and asked the assistant for a pet wasp. She told him some-what disdainfully that they didn't stock wasps and, in any case, they weren't creatures that people would want to cultivate as pets. 'But,' said Chic. 'You've got two in the window.'

CHIC described a visit, possibly imagined, to the Olympic Games. He was taking a leisurely stroll in the environs of the stadium when he espied a man coming towards him, dressed in a T-shirt and shorts and carrying a long stick over his shoulder. Chic said: 'Excuse me, are you a pole vaulter?'

'No,' replied the athlete. 'I'm a German. And by the way, how did you know my name?'

A CLASSIC Chic Murray story concerns an attempt to find lodgings in a typically welcoming Scottish seaside town. He knocked on the door of a B&B establishment. The landlady opened an upstairs window and asked brusquely what he wanted. 'I'd like to stay here,' he said. 'Well, stay there,' she replied and closed the window.

SOME London-based television people didn't know quite what to make of Chic Murray. Chic was being interviewed on the Simon Dee chat show and the host was trying to put Chic down by repeating his answers, translating the Scottish accent into BBC-received pronunciation.

But Chic had a spot of revenge waiting in the wings. When asked about variety acts he remembered, Chic reminisced about a high-wire troupe. 'They were billed as Lunt, Hunt, and Cunningham,' he said in his plummiest voice and waited deadpan for a response. The verbal challenge went unanswered. 'Lunt, Hunt, and Cunningham,' he repeated with slow emphasis.

The interview ended with Mr Dee, head in hands, face down on the table.

THE word surreal only begins to describe Chic Murray's sense of humour. He took the opportunity, when appearing on the TV comedy quiz show *Jokers Wild*, to push this surrealism to the limit. Asked to discourse on the subject of the seaside, he said: 'I won the pools once, and I said to my mother, "Ma, I've won the pools. What would you like? You can have anything you want." "Oh, son, I'd like to see the sea. I've never seen the sea." So I took her to the seaside, put her on a deckchair and went away. I came back after two weeks and said to my mother, "Well ma, what do you think of the sea?" She replied, "Is that all it does?"'

Another joke which mystified the *Jokers Wild* audience: 'Can I have a bar of green soap?' asks Chic of the

APOLOGY

In J.J. Campbell's Advert last week we erroneously printed the phrase "Catch us with our trousers down" when we should have said "Catch us with our prices down". We apologise unreservedly for any embarrassment this may have caused J.J. CAMPBELL assistant in a chemist's shop. 'I'm sorry, we only have yellow soap,' she replies. 'That's okay,' Chic reassures her, 'I've got my bike outside.' It also mystified Diary readers who telephoned in their scores for an explanation. I told them it was an attempt by Chic Murray to question the essential nature of humour. Some of them even believed me.

CHIC was famous for his conversations with his doctor. 'Tell me,' asked the GP, 'are you disturbed by improper thoughts during the night?' 'No,' Chic replied. 'I actually enjoy them.'

'STRIP,' said the doctor. 'Where will I hang my clothes,' asked Chic.

'Just put them on top of mine,' replied the doctor.

'WHAT'S your problem?' asked the doctor. 'I've got butterflies in my stomach,' said Chic. 'Have you eaten anything recently?' inquired the doc. 'Butterflies, actually.'

TALES abound about Chic's ability to while away his daytime hours drinking coffee and distracting the staff in offices where he happened to know the boss. He was a regular visitor to the office of a Glasgow entertainments agency. One summer afternoon, while Chic was there passing the time reading the office's supply of daily newspapers, the work of the office was further disturbed by a loud and persistent bluebottle. There

was a sudden bang as a rolled-up *Glasgow Herald* brought the bluebottle's short life to an end.

A deadly hush fell over the office staff who all looked at Chic. His response: 'Sorry. Was it someone's pet?'

Harry Lymburn of the Tait and McLay advertising agency in Glasgow recalled that Chic was no stranger to their offices, mostly to pass the time of day with his pal, the late Jack McLay whom he referred to as the Wee Man.

'On one such occasion, having asked Jean our receptionist if the Wee Man was in, he was told a white lie because Jack was busy meeting a deadline for a client and Chic's visits were known to be anything but short.'

Chic replied that this was not a problem. He would wait for the Wee Man's return. Settled down with a cup of coffee, Chic proceeded to keep the entire front-office staff off their work. Some considerable time later, Jean excused herself, went into Jack's office and explained the situation.

Jack's predicament was that there was no way out of the office without being spotted by Chic. He resolved the predicament by opening his office window and dreeping (good old Glasgow word, there) a full storey into the back garden, climbing the railings, and coming in the front door to greet Chic.

MICHAEL Glancy of Bearsden remembered being introduced to Chic by a mutual friend. Being young and somewhat in awe of the great man, Mr Glancy stumbled for words and could only say: 'Hello, Chic, how are you?' Putting the young man at his ease, Chic replied: 'I'm fine, apart from the odd touch of diarrhoea.'

CHIC, buying an Underground ticket at Hillhead, enquired: 'By the way, is there a buffet car on this train?'

'No, sorry sir.'

'Well, is there a buffet car on the next train, then?'

'No sir. There are no buffet cars on any of our trains, sir.'

'Christ, I'll be starving by the time I get to Merkland Street.'

THE Rev. Eric Hudson of Bearsden recalled how Chic related to him the story of his father's funeral. Totally deadpan, Chic told how his mother was a Cherokee Indian (from Greenock) and when his father died she wanted him to have a traditional Cherokee funeral. This involved building a pyre in the back garden and putting the deceased person's dearest possession on to the flames.

So on went Chic's dad's wee dug. After the fire died down and the remains were being gathered together, Chic's mother, he said, picked up a piece of bone. 'Pity the wee dug's no' here,' she said sadly. 'He loved a good bone.'

CHIC on being commiserated with after slipping on an icy pavement and falling on his bahookey: 'Did you slip on the ice?' asked a perspicacious passer-by. 'No. I've got a bar of chocolate in my back pocket and I'm trying to break it,' he replied.

A NEIGHBOUR asked if he could use Chic's lawnmower. 'Certainly,' he replied, 'but please don't take it out of my garden.'

CHIC'S remark as he fell from a bus: 'It's alright. I was getting off anyway.'

CHIC'S aside during a rambling story about how he had spent the day: 'I was making tea in my pyjamas. I must get a teapot.'

CHIC, in a shop buying soap, was asked: 'Do you want it scented?' 'No thanks,' he said. 'Wrap it up and I'll take it with me.'

'I WALKED into the bedroom – the curtains were drawn but the furniture was real.'

CHIC speaking of a trip to Helensburgh in the days when every chemist's shop had a penny-in-the-slot weighing machine in the doorway: 'It's a wonderfully exciting place is Helensburgh. Full of entertainment. I weighed myself twice.'

CHIC was once standing at a bus stop eating a pie supper when he was joined in the queue by a lady with a small dog. The said small dog, incited by the aroma of Chic's al fresco snack, was jumping up and down attempting to gain access to his pie and chips.

'Would you like me to throw him a

bit?' Chic asked her. She replied that her dog would like that very much so Chic picked up the dog and, so the story goes, but we can't believe Chic would hurt a wee dug, threw him a bit . . .

CHIC went into a butcher's shop. 'Have you got pig's trotters?' he asked the friendly butcher who replied that he had. 'I'll have a pound of mince then, Porky . . .'

CHIC was driving past a farmhouse when he ran over a cockerel. Conscience stricken, he picked up the deceased bird and knocked on the door. 'I'm afraid I've just killed your cockerel and would like to replace him,' he told the farmer's wife. 'Fair enough,' she said. 'The hens are round the back.'

CHIC often told how he was on a bus in his boyhood Greenock, accompanied by his father. The bus ran out of control, down a hill and crashed into a wall. 'Were you hurt?' his audience would inevitably ask. 'No, but father had the presence of mind to kick me in the face.'

MEN AND WOMEN

THIS chap arrives home from work to find his wife rubbing cream into her breasts. It is guaranteed to increase the size of her bust, she tells him. How much did it cost, he asks. £79. 'Whit,' he exclaims. 'Why didn't you just get a daud o' toilet roll and rub it between your cleavage?'

'Will it work?' the wife asks.

'Well, it's worked for your arse,' the uncouth chap replies.

DEPT of Public House Folklore: We heard distressing details of how a Govan chap was rusticated from his favourite pub. Having discovered that his wife was having an affair, he tracked the philanderer to the pub where he found the man making a phone call. He proceeded to attack him with a machete. The victim suffered severe wounds to his arm. The telephone cable was severed. The attacker was barred by the publican for 'putting the phone out of order'.

THE landlord of a West Highland hostelry was carrying a box of empty bottles into the back yard when he discovered his wife in a compromising situation with a customer. Deeply hurt by this infidelity, the landlord shouted to the man: 'You bastard, you're barred!' As mine host retreated from the scene, he realised that the chap was by far his biggest-spending customer and added: 'For a month!'

DURING the festive season chaps, emboldened by a sweet sherry or two at the office party, are to be found trying to chat up the temp from accounts. We heard of one Lothario – in Barrhead, of all romantic locations – who has set a standard of sweet talk to which the rest of us can only aspire. 'You know,' he told the chubby but comely object of his desires, 'you don't sweat very much for a fat person.'

A Lanarkshire lady of a certain age was on the receiving end of this scintillating patter: 'You know, you're not as old as you look.'

ANOTHER festive-season chat-up line. Diner to comely waitress as she pours cream over his pudding: 'Tell me, dear, what are you and your jug of cream doing later?' Waitress: 'I don't know about the jug of cream but I'm goin' hame to my man.'

114

OTHER sensitive appraisals of the female sex included:

'You're lookin' a million dollars the night, hen. A' green and wrinkly.'

'Haw, sweetheart, ah love the frock. Did ye huv much bother sneakin' it oot the museum?'

'You've got really interestin' eyes. In fact the right wan's that interestin', yer left wan keeps lookin' at it.'

'Huv youse two came oot fur a drink an' left Cinders in hersel again?'

EVEN worse than your average male's chat-up lines are the discussions they have with their mates the day after a conquest. Like: 'Ah widnae say she was a big girl, but her middle name wis Orca and Greenpeace are lookin' for her tae tow her back oot to sea.'

WITH some trepidation, the Diary explored the subject of lady motorists. Like the one who was asked if she knew that she had driven all the way home with a flat tyre. Yes, she said, she had noticed before she drove off. But she thought it would be OK since the tyre was only flat on the bottom.

A WOMAN came to a garage counter and told the storeman that she had just bought a second-hand Austin A40. And could she buy a longer dip-stick because the one she had wouldn't reach the oil.

115

A LANARKSHIRE father told of the time his daughter noticed her car was low on petrol as she drove home. Ten minutes later she was stopped by the polis and asked why, at 11 p.m., she was driving without lights. She replied: 'I am nearly out of petrol so I switched off the lights to save fuel.'

A LADY caught by the polis speeding through an area signposted as an accident black spot gave the eminently reasonable excuse: 'Well, you don't want to dawdle through a danger area, do you?'

A LITTLE old lady was driving along the hard shoulder of the motorway at about 15 miles an hour. An AA van, thinking that she was in some kind of trouble, drew up in front of her. The AA man got out and spoke to her. The little, old, and by this time angry, lady asked: 'Why do you think there's anything wrong?' The AA man informed her that she was driving on the hard shoulder. 'Oh,' said the little old lady. 'I always drive in this lane. I find there's not much traffic in it.'

WE heard many a tale of disaster involving people driving a new company car for the first time. A young lady, who will remain nameless, kept up the tradition in an incident in Dundee. She came out of a side-street and smacked into a passing, occupied hearse. The funeral procession was brought to a halt and, to avoid any distress to the bereaved, the hearse driver suggested that the young lady join the end of the procession of cars to the cemetery where details of insurance could be exchanged. Thus she came to phone her office with this message: 'I've been in an accident and I'm at the cemetery but the person in the other car was dead when I hit him.'

WARNING: This joke may upset wimmin.

Q: Why do sumo wrestlers shave their legs?
A: So that they won't be mistaken for feminists.

In mitigation we should say that this joke came to us via a really well-known feminist. You probably know her fine. The one with the sense of humour.

THE scene is a shop in Paisley which deals in handbags and other accessories. Enter a wee wumman who wants to buy a handbag. 'A blue handbag,' she tells the assistant.
'What shade of blue?' asks the assistant.
'The same colour as my budgie,' she replies, producing a photograph of said budgie.

THE ladies' toilet of the Speaker's Corner bar and bistro, Sauchiehall Street, Glasgow, has a vending machine which, for £2, dispenses a package containing two tampons, two condoms, and four paracetamol. A handy little something for the week-

116

end which would seem to cover all eventualities.

ANENT the above item on the ladies' toilet vending machine which dispenses an all-encompassing package of condoms, tampons, and paracetamol, a former Heriot-Watt student told us that when she was a fresher at said yooni she was issued with a similarly intriguing juxtaposition of goodies. It was a poke (if you'll pardon the expression) containing a packet of condoms and a pot noodle. For a romantic night just add music, candlelight, champagne, and some boiling water.

FROM Cowglen golf course in Glasgow, we hear of two chaps who were waved through by two ladies who were halfway up the eighth fairway. The ladies proceeded to walk back to the tee. As the gents passed, they thanked the ladies for their courtesy and asked if they had lost both balls. 'No,' one of them replied sheepishly. 'We forgot to drive.'

GLESCA

GLASGOW has changed in the last decade or so with the advent of Mayfest, the *annus mirabilis* of the European Year of Culture, and the general growth of the city's arts industry. Glasgow's lifestyle has changed too. Here is a list of the ways a typical Glasgow working chap was then and the way he is now.

THEN:

Job description: Welder in Govan shipyard and part-time comedian.

House: One-room tenement flat in Partick, shared with wife and four children.

Breakfast: Two rashers of bacon, fried egg, black pudding, and a potato scone, all in a City Bakeries roll.

Lunch: Spam sandwiches (Mondays and Wednesdays) and corned-beef sandwiches (Tuesdays and Thursdays); Fridays, a pie and four pints of heavy in pub.

Dinner: Actually, it was called your tea in those days and was corned-beef fritters (Mondays and Wednesdays) and Spam fritters (Tuesdays and Thursdays); Fridays, another pie and eight pints of heavy in the pub.

Method of transport: Glasgow Corporation bus; no motor car.

NOW:

Job description: Area liaison inward investment executive (business and the arts division) with Govan Enterprise and part-time comedian.

House: Bachelor studio flat in Partick; wife and four children living in the bungalow in Bearsden.

Breakfast: Two slices of prosciutto, Eggs Benedict, *un morceau de boudin noir* and a potato scone, all in a City Bakeries croissant.

Lunch: Glass of Highland Spring, Ryvita and cottage cheese (Mondays to Thursdays); Fridays, Spam roll and a Spritzer in pub.

Dinner: Now called dinner and consists, Mondays to Thursdays, of any low-fat, low-salt Marks and Spencer meal for one, washed down with Earl Grey tea. Fridays, pie and eight pints of Spritzer in the pub.

Method of transport: Strathclyde Bus; politically correct way to travel.

118

Girlfriend: Senga, waitress in the works canteen.

Problem with girlfriend: His wife has just found out.

Favourite team: Celtic.
Last time he was in a fight: When some idiot stole his bottle of Lanliq at a party in Partick.

Idea of a good night out: Spend a tenner on a meal in an Italian restaurant and then on to a country and western music club.
Ambition: To get out of the shipyards.

Girlfriend: Miranda, drama student who works part-time as a waitress with outside catering company which provides executive buffets at Govan Enterprise.
Problem with girlfriend: His daughter, who's in Miranda's class at drama school, has just found out.
Favourite team: Boston Celtics.
Last time he was in a fight: When some idiot stole his bottle of Marques de Caceres gran reserva Rioja at a dinner party in Partick and replaced it with a bottle of Lanliq.
Idea of a good night out: Take in a concert by an Italian tenor and then for supper to a Tex-Mex cantina.

Ambition: To attract the shipbuilding industry back to Govan.

119

DUNDEE

THE Diary was pleased to adopt Dundee, on the silvery Tay, for the duration of its Oxtercentenary (800th birthday to youse), and to gather fascinating facts about the place we affectionately came to know as Clootie City.

BINGO players will be familiar with such cries as '88, two fat ladies' and 'key of the door, 21'. In Dundee the bingo callers were wont to cry, to the consternation of women present, '76. Was she worth it? Seven and six.'

THERE was a famous Clootie City costermonger who was regularly heard to cry: 'Onions! Genuine Spanish onions! Nane o' yer foreign muck here!'

DUNDEE'S Labour clubs collapsed amidst a financial débâcle with all sorts of allegations of criminal activity. One of the people involved received a communication containing two bullets and note with a Mafia-style warning: to whit, the single word *Omertà*. The word, in typical Clootie City literary tradition, was in fact misspelt. It appeared on the note as 'O'Merta'. No doubt it was from the Irish Mafia.

A WORKERS' meeting was called by the management at Dundee's Michelin factory in an attempt to persuade the workforce to adopt a new shift system in which they would lose the right to have Saturday and Sunday off each week. You would still have a 'weekend' off, a management negotiator explained, except that it would not be Saturday and Sunday every week. One worker, a well-known sage, was asked by the management chap to explain why he was shaking his head. 'Am I to understand,' said the sage, 'that a Tuesday could be like a Saturday and a Wednesday like a Sunday?' 'Exactly,' said the management man, pleased to have made the big breakthrough in understanding. 'Can you tell me how I'm going to get a *Sunday Post* on a Wednesday?' the worker replied. The proposal was rejected.

NO less a person than Ken Sykora, doyen broadcaster and presenter of Radio Scotland's *Eater's Digest*, told us that the chip was invented in Dundee. Not the microchip, the fried chip. Mr Sykora unearthed this fascinating fact in an interview with Kinross hotelier Terry Doyle. Mr

Doyle insisted that the chip was created in Dundee by his great grandfather, Frenchman Edouard Dejernier. Monsieur Dejernier moved to Dundee in the 1870s, where he started up a chain of fish restaurants. He introduced the fritter and the 'finger' which later became known simply as the chip. His tattie innovation was carried abroad by visiting sailors. The delicacy was known as Frenchie's Fries, now better known as French fries.

ONE of Dundee's most famous sons is Lieutenant Montgomery Scott. He is better known as Scottie, as in 'Beam me up, Scottie'. Yes, the cantankerous engineer in *Star Trek* hails from the city of the Tay. This information can be verified in an episode in which Scottie fantasises about being a Highland laird. He reminisces: 'Och, I wish I was back in my native Dundee . . .'

A CLUE to the psyche of Dundee may be found in how Clootie City celebrated the anniversary of VE Day. The great and the good in Dundee decided in their infinite wisdom that the returning soldiery, after six years of war, could not be trusted to conduct themselves in a manner fitting to this great occasion, so all the pubs were ordered to stay shut that night. There were no riots following this momentous decision, but there were a great many dumbfounded, depressed and drouthy demobbed Dundonians dandering

dejectedly around the streets of dry Dundee.

JIM McLean, former manager, chairman, and God of Dundee United, in a way epitomises the city. Mr McLean has a reputation for having an uncompromising nature. This was enhanced by a tale about his reaction to a letter from a young fan. The young Arab (as United fans are called) put pen to paper, as is every paying punter's right, to inform Mr McLean that he thought some of his team selections were wrong. The letter duly went into Mr McLean's in-tray. After

121

Ayatollah McLean had dealt with the day's business (torturing apprentices, rebuilding the stadium, checking the Tannadice bank balance) he set off home, stopping on his way at the address from which the letter had come. He knocked on the door and asked the lady of the house if the boy was in. The boy duly appeared to be told by Mr McLean: 'Look, I pick the team.'

HOW do you recognise a Dundee police car? Simple. It's got a roof rack. This is a reference to one of the less glorious chapters in the history of Dundee's finest. Folklore has it that the Dundee force is the only one in the country that had to call out the day shift to the night shift. The incident occurred in the early 1970s when some of the night-shift boys in blue succumbed to temptation while investigating a burglary at a local pub, The Rowan Tree. Local urchins had much fun in the ensuing months by singing 'Rowan tree, Oh rowan tree' to passing bobbies.

THE *Sun* newspaper reported under the heading 'Randy Ravers Flock To Cammy's Pit Of Passion', the opening of a Dundee club where sex was the motif. On entering he premises, clubbers were confronted by a giant phallic symbol; statues with Madonnaesque pointed boobs; a bar held up by bare-bottomed, knickerless, stockinged ladies' legs; and if that wasn't enough to move the earth, a specially woven sperm-patterned car-

pet. The steamy decor of the passion pit was lost on one Dundonian lass, who told the *Sun*: 'I didn't realise sex was the theme until someone pointed it out to me.'

IN Dundeespeak the number two is pronounced twaa. An example of this comes from the Dundee soldier who returned from war service in France. Asked how he liked that country, he replied: 'It's great. Every time you ask for twaa eggs, ye get three.'

THIS tale concerns a job which Dundee Council put out to tender. Three firms put in bids. An Aberdeen company offered to do the job for £3,000 on the basis of £1,000 for materials, £1,000 for labour, and £1,000 profit margin. An Edinburgh firm put in a bid of £6,000 – with £2,000 each earmarked for materials, labour and profit. A Dundee firm put in a tender of £9,000 and was duly invited to meet a senior council official to give a breakdown of its estimate. 'Simple,' said the Dundee businessman. '£3,000 to you, £3,000 to me and £3,000 for the Aberdeen boys to do the work.'

DUNDEE cops were conducting inquiries in the Hawkhill area and one of the interviewees was a Dundee District Council cleansing department employee whose beat took in the locus of the crime. He was approached by one of Tayside's finest who had surmised that the street-sweeper might have seen something

of value to their investigation. 'What is your name?' he asked. The cleansing operative told him. 'Address?' This information was duly given. 'Occupation?' the polisman asked. The roadsweeper looked at his dustcart, looked at his cleansing department uniform and said to the policeman: 'Actually, I'm a brain surgeon at the Dundee Royal Infirmary.' The police were not amused and took the unfortunate scaffie down to the nick where he was kept in custody for an hour for obstructing police inquiries. He was released with a warning 'not to be stupid in future'. Unrepentant, he replied: 'Well, you started it.'

JAMES McDonald, a famous son of Dundee, died last year in Los Angeles. Both Dundee Labour MPs, Ernie Ross and John McAllion, put down an early-day motion at the House of Commons to ensure he did not go unmourned. The motion read: 'This House regrets the passing of Mr James McDonald, born in Dundee 84 years ago, who brought pleasure to millions for more than 40 years as the voice of Mickey Mouse and who provided the yodelling, whistling and sneezing for Walt Disney's classic 1937 cartoon film *Snow White and the Seven Dwarfs*, and expresses its sincere sympathy for his widow, Roberta.' It matters little that Mr McDonald's parents emigrated from Dundee when he was only a month old. The city by the Tay needs all the famous sons it can get.

A TAYSIDE linguist informed us that the accent of the people of Clootie City is characterised by an extraneous Y at the end of words. Thus, he tells, it is not usual for a Dundee tradesman to announce that he is 'awa' tae dae a wee job-y'.

ONE of Dundee's most famous politicians was Mr Edward 'Neddy' Scrymgeour, the Prohibition candidate who unseated Winston Churchill from his Dundee seat. As you will gather from his ticket, Neddy was a fierce critic of the drink. He had to suffer continual barracking from sundry drunks at his election meetings. Undeterred, he would warn these imbibers that, come prohibition, all the ales and ardent spirits in Dundee would be emptied into the River Tay. Equally undeterred, a gang of the said imbibers at one meeting reacted to this news by singing the hymn: 'Yes, we'll gather at the river . . .'

MALAPROPAGATION

MALAPROPISMS continued to be a feature of the Diary's mailbag. Like:

The man explaining his son's absence from work: 'Jimmy'll be aff fur a couple o' days. He's choked up with the diarrhoea.'

The angry woman who said of the object of her fury that she 'would have his heid for garters'.

A chap called Davy who, on hearing of a bereavement, offered his 'heartiest condolences'. To Davy, problems were like 'runner aff a dug's back'. He was often 'blue wi' envy'. Sadly, Davy is now deceased. Or as he might have put it himself: 'Doon in heaven, noo.'

A lady discussing her daughter's health: 'Our Rose got out of the hospital for Christmas, but she's real poorly. She's got to go back in next week for one of them barrow meals.'

The middle-aged woman from Springburn who confided to a close friend that her husband's sexual demands appeared to be at an end, because he had become 'impertinent'.

The radio commentator, who, during the latest appearance of Halley's Comet, described it as a 'distinct blur'.

The councillor who opined during an education debate that Strathclyde region might 'find itself up a gum tree without a paddle'.

The German businessman who, when giving a talk in English, used the unfortunate phrase 'Early to bed and up with the cock'.

A chap who boasted about his son's prowess at the swimming baths: 'He can swim like a lintie.'

A granny who described how an audacious thief stole her purse right there in the street 'when it was pitch daylight'.

The woman whose friend got a job as a 'vigilante' at last year's Higher examinations.

A perplexed office manager: 'How would I know what's going to happen next week? I'm not Houdini.'

An office telephonist responsible for such pearls as:
- She smells like a tart's brewery.
- I'm as dry as a boat.
- Don't worry your cotton-headed socks about it.
- This behaviour reeks of 1994.

The girl, talking about a colleague's many and varied outside interests, who said: 'That man's got a pie everywhere!'

The chap from Kilmarnock who revealed to his workmates the bad news that he was suffering from 'glocamora' in one eye.

The young female patient who told her doctor: 'You know how erotic I am with my periods.' Also slightly medical is the story of the gent who had spent a fortune on his girls' education and upbringing, and announced to his friends that he had 'very costive daughters'.

The manager of an unnamed factory in Dumbarton who had been sent on a course on ergonomics and the production line. On his return he received a complaint that a certain procedure was giving a female worker severe backache and he announced that he would be 'out to have a right good look at her posterior'.

The sad story of the young couple who split up 'before the marriage was even consumed'.

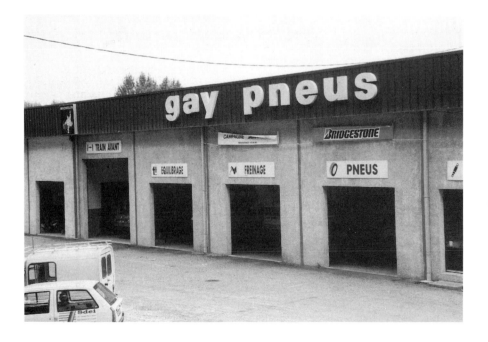

The party that turned out to be a 'damp squid'.

The lady shopper who liked to go 'bruising' along Sauchiehall Street.

The councillor who, asked to give his opinion on two candidates for a promotion, said the first 'was a man of a different caliper'.

The Celtic fans who gave their team 'a helluva barracading'.

The Scout troop leader who told parents there would be a '£5 decapitation fee' for each boy.

The factory forman who had continually warned the apprentices about 'all corrugating in the one place'.

This criticism of a neighbour: 'She thinks she's the Queen's knees.'

The angry retort: 'That's right, kick the teeth from under me.'

Agnes from Anniesland who would introduce pieces of family gossip with the phrase 'This is without a word of truth.'

The old lady whose nephew had been involved in a 'fricassee' in a pub.

The old gentleman who was said to suffer from agoraphobia: 'Y'know, he's frightened of outer space.'

The man who, after the General Election, moaned that we were now stuck with the 'quo vadis'.

The talented wordsmith who described his workplace as being like the 'Black Hole of Kentucky'.

The woman who complained about the threat to her health from her workmates' 'passion smoking'.

The man whose favourite song was 'Mairi's Sweating'.

The man who used to drive along a 'jewelled garageway'.

The woman who, when requiring help, announced: 'I've only got two pairs of hands.'

The woman complaining about her new kitchen: 'There's no room to skin a cat.'

The man who helpfully suggested to a tourist: 'It's only five minutes' walk if you run.'

The man who commented on the absent-mindedness of a friend: 'He's got a memory the size of a sieve.'

The manager who said: 'There's a vulture up there watching me like a hawk!' The same man also said: 'Don't axe yer grind wi' me, fella!'

The proprietor of the small electrical shop who is frequently asked for 'Durex batteries'.

The Strathaven lady watching scenes on the TV news of the Scottish team returning from Sweden after another magnificent international footballing failure: 'Aye, they sure went out in a puff of glory.'

The new granny who said her daughter had a forced delivery 'because her pelmet was too small'.

The old lady at the supermarket checkout who, when paying her bill of £4.18, fetched four £1 notes from her purse and then asked the assistant to 'wait a minute, hen, and I'll gie ye some of this stramash out of my purse'.

The grandmother who said she wouldn't buy a newspaper with tennis player Billie Jean King on the front because she was one of those 'Elizabethans'.

The Glasgow office girl who informed her colleagues that she would be preparing for a social engagement by 'going to have her nails manacled and her cubicles pushed back'.

The rugby player who was tackled by a full-back at the opposition line but his 'impotence' took him over.

The woman whose boyfriend caught 'fluorosis of the liver'.

The wee girl who said her mum had just come out of hospital 'after having her second autopsy but they still found nothing wrong'.

A true story from an epilepsy sufferer who was confiding in a friend about coping with his condition. 'The trouble with being an epileptic is that you become invisible to other people,' he said. 'I know,' his pal replied. 'There's still a lot of astigmatism attached to it.'

The man training for the Glasgow Half-Marathon who declared himself 'as fit as a fish'.

The sage who declared that he was appalled at the cost to the European Parliament of translating their deliberations into all the different tongues and had the perfect solution: 'Why don't they all speak the same language – that eldorado.'

The school teacher confronted with a mountain of paperwork who sighed: 'There goes another Babylonian rain forest.'

The woman genealogical researcher who had succeeded in finding an elusive forefather in the Register Office where her siblings had failed. She announced: 'It will be a bee in my bonnet when the others see this.'

The job applicant who said, after a difficult interview: 'I didn't expect the Spanish requisition.'

The Glasgow lady who opted for some alternative medicine at 'that home of the pathetics hospital in Great Western Road'.

Overheard in a coffee shop in London:
Her: 'He's a bit of a dark fish.'
Him: 'Don't you mean a slippery horse?'

The salesman who, upon spotting an approaching colleague, said: 'Aye, here he comes. Nae smoke without punch!'

The chap who described a devious friend as having 'more faces than the hands of the toon clock'.

The youngster who had not quite grasped the basics of playground debating skills or even a command of basic swearing. He disagreed with a member of his peer group who, he claimed, was 'talking quiche'.

The woman who said her brother-in-law had 'never been anything but a snake in the ointment'.

The girl who told how a rival in pursuit of her boyfriend made 'a bee-hive right for him'.

The neighbour who boasted that her brother had just bought a new car with one of those 'catholic converters'.

The woman when commenting on some newly built houses said they were 'packed in cheek by bowel'.

The man who said that the after-dinner speaker has 'waxed effluent'.

The millionaire who was described as an industrial 'magnet'.

The man who described his associates as a 'henspeckled bunch'.

The man in the bar who said his employer was offering him 'a PLO cruise'.

The girl who said of a financially troubled company that the worst day was when they brought 'the liquidisers in'. Presumably she meant the retrievers.

The Rangers fan commenting on his team's lack of penetration on the flanks in the absence of Gary Stevens: 'We're missing him like a sore thumb.'

The girl who said: 'I know a chap who went to Israel to live on a kebab for two years.'

The mother who said that a relative had 'cried fox' too often.

The trade-union official at a meeting with the health board who claimed: 'The Sword of Domestos is hanging over our members' heads.'

The mother-in-law who enjoys a cup of tea because 'it fair survives you'.

The Wishaw lady who was discussing the merits of the various brands of lager and asked her daughter if she had ever tasted 'that Castlemilk four X'.

The woman on her Highland holiday who had a 'panasonic view' of the mountains from her hotel window.

The old lady on the train to Edinburgh who pointed out they were near Auld Reekie by saying: 'Look! There's the Jenner's Suppository'.

The man who took a dram every night and slept 'like a Trojan'.

The foreman in the parks department who had to cope with student summer workers and who often accused them of being 'too smart with your O levels and your C levels'.

The woman in the fabric shop who complained she couldn't see the shade of her curtain material because of the 'effervescent lights'.

The girl whose sister was going into hospital for a 'Bavarian meal'.

The director who warned his staff not to go 'off in a tandem'.

The chap who went to Moscow but found himself totally confused by the 'acrylic alphabet'.

The gent who said he saw a drunk man 'lying prosperous in the gutter'.

The man who said his holiday was a 'total fiesta'.

The young police constable, fresh from training school and anxious to get the full story of a road accident, who asked the hospital doctor: 'This broken leg. Has the victim fractured his tibia or his labia?'

The lady who waited in her car to join the funeral 'corsage'.

The lady whose favourite soap was 'Imperial Lather'.

The woman of whom it was said: 'Every time she opens her mouth she shoots herself in the foot.'

The teenager who had seen a TV programme on the slimmer's disease: 'Aye, it's terrible that anaglypta nervosa.'

The woman who realised she'd mixed up her words and said: 'Oh dear, is that me doing a Mrs Malathorp?'

The RAC man who informed a motorist: 'Your battery's as flat as a dodo.'

The lady who commented that the man next door had bought a 'Puguenot' motor car.

The man who was jumped on by a 'Karachi expert'.

The dear old lady who says her daughter has two dogs: 'One a Corgi, the other a Datsun.'

The salesman who when finalising details of the purchase of a mobile office was told his customer wanted it 'in perpetuity'. That could be a problem, he said. He'd quoted for it being in Yoker.

The builder who told his boss that he couldn't go up heights because he suffered from 'vertebrae'.

The manager who arrived at the metallurgy laboratory of a large factory looking for the report on 'the non-ferocious metals'.

The woman 'who's not in the phone book. She's hysterectomy.'

The gent who declared: 'It's like getting blood out of a dead horse' and 'You're rubbing blood into the wound'.

The woman who tired of being taken for granted by her family and yelled: 'I'm fed up being treated like a dormouse!'

The man who, when asked to perform miracles, chided: 'Do you think I've got a genie I can rub?'

The local businessman who gave in to yuppiedom and bought 'one o' thae celluloid phones'.

The chap in the restaurant who informed the waitress: 'We'll just have the soup and the pudding, lassie. We've no time for the intercourse.'

A shipyard worker, the victim of a

DONNACHIE'S BAR, Cobh

Due to the sad death of Paddy, the Bar, to all intents and purposes, will remain closed during our grief; but so as not to inconvenience our esteemed customers, the door will remain ajar. 'Tis what Paddy wanted.
Thank you, **DONNACHIE FAMILY**

practical joke, who vowed: 'I'll get you for that. As sure as God made toffee apples, I'll get you.'

THE Gorbals lady who done good moved to a more highly rated socio-economic area of the South Side of Glasgow. Whitecraigs, even. At a social get-together, the lady was on the fringe of a conversation and overheard one of her neighbours talking about his latest acquisition – a boathouse. 'We've got a boathouse as well,' she chipped in. 'We bought our house 12 years ago.'

THEN there was the reader who, after a week of torture on the Cambridge diet had produced no weight loss, was told by her minder: 'Your weight does tend to flatulate from time to time.'

THE following *bons mots* fell from one Glasgow office worker's lips like birds of a feather:

- It's a Catch-66 situation.
- He was wearing a polar-neck sweater.
- He's as merry as a kite.
- He's worth his weight in salt.
- This is the crutch of the situation.
- I have been given complete cordon blanche.

• See you soon, no doubt, if not before.

ON the holiday front, there was the man who regaled his workmates with details of how he travelled through France overnight by train 'on a courgette'.

SOME pearls of wisdom just come straight out of the blue. Like the personnel manager who liked to tell applicants who had made the short leet that 'the trees are beginning to thin and your picture's definitely on the piano'.

FROM Stonehaven we heard of a chap whose love life was tangled, to say the least. In fact, as one local put it, he was involved in a 'fromage à trois'.

SOME Glaswegians go to great lengths to avoid speaking a' wrang. Occasionally they mangle perfectly good words. Like the woman who had been off work suffering from the bile. Or 'the boil', as she informed workmates.

MUSIC is a rich source of examples of people what get it wrong. Like the child who sang fervently each Christmas about a 'wean in a anger'. Or the grown-up whose rendition of the Jim Reeves song *He'll Have to Go* always began: 'Put the jukebox a little closer to the phone . . .'

The member of a Highland district council who fell out with a troublesome constituent, gave him 'a piece of my tongue' and sent him away 'with his tail between his teeth'.

The following solecisms are from a larger collection of the pearls of wisdom as uttered by a chap who works in a West of Scotland whisky company. Our informant insisted that the whisky is not a factor:
• I've spoken to every dog and their granny.
• It's an ill wind that blows your granny off a bus.
• Any ship in a storm.
• Old Mother Cupboard.
• Speak now or forever hold your water.

AS good as malapropism, in the Diary's opinion, is when two well-known sayings are combined, such as:
• The woman who 'screamed blue-arsed murder'.
• The politician who warned of 'buying two peas in a poke'.
• The chap who knew a certain secret because 'a wee bird dropped something in my ear'.

NOT quite a malaprop but very close is the story of a young Coatbridge lad who was under the impression for many years that Doris Day sang a number with the chorus: 'Kiss her arse, her arse . . .'

NOT a malaprop but definitely a misspeak is this, attributed to a ScotRail inspector who had been asked to check the conditions in the gentleman's restroom: 'Thae toilets ur a pure disgrace,' he reported. 'It's like a shithoose in there.'

QUOTE UNQUOTE

THE Scots have a cheery way of welcoming German tourists to these shores. The German in question was upstairs in a bus in Edinburgh. He remarked loudly that smoking was such a disgusting habit. This comment was obviously aimed at the elderly gent in a bunnet who was smoking a pipe. The smoking bunnet replied: 'The effan smoke didny seem to bother yiz at Auschwitz.'

A PUBLIC inquiry at the City Halls in Glasgow heard an application by a mining firm who wished to operate an open-cast mine on the outskirts of Easterhouse. One of the concerns voiced by anxious locals was that 'settlement ponds' which would have to be dug would pose a danger to children in the area. No problem, said a company spokesman. A wall-and-chain-link fence 17 feet high would be built round the ponds. 'You don't ken the weans frae Easterhouse,' was the comment from one of the locals in the hall.

GLASGOW continues to welcome tourists in its own peculiar way. An English chap was overheard in the bar of the Boswell Hotel enthusing about the selection of real ales on tap. He was particularly impressed by the MacLays. 'Where is MacLays from?' he asked the barman. The barman, obviously enrolled in the Chic Murray school of humour, replied: 'By the look of you, from Paddy's Market.' Laughter from locals, bemused look from tourist.

GREAT Tannoy Announcements of Our Time. During a speedway match in Peterborough involving Glasgow Tigers, the following information was broadcast: 'Would the driver of the yellow Vauxhall Nova in the carpark please note that his Alsatian dog has just switched the windscreen wipers on.'

RICHARD Stobbs of the Mount Florida Community Council commenting on the subject of football fans' misbehaviour in the vicinity of Hampden Park on big match days: 'Our gardens are constantly being used as toilets and litter bins. I personally have had my fill . . .'

NOTICE in the church bulletin of the Sacred Heart Church in Carndonagh, County Donegal: 'Cemetery

134

Blessing: The annual ceremony of blessing the graves in the cemetery will be held at five p.m. on Sunday 18 August. Please ensure that your grave is neat and tidy for the occasion.'

GREAT Tannoy Announcements of Our Time II. A dreary Monday morning on the Glasgow Underground at Govan was greatly enlivened by the following announcement: 'Would driver Singh please phone control and we'll tell him where his train is.'

WHAT do you get if you cross a Rottweiler and a Labrador? A dog which scares the shit out of you and then runs away with the toilet paper.

EILEEN McCallum rose even higher in the Diary's estimation when she accepted her award as Scotland's actress of the year at a Bafta Scotland ceremony. In her wee speech after receiving her Baffie (or whatever they're called), she said: 'Oh dear. If I knew I was going to win, I would have bleached my moustache.'

MIDLOTHIAN District Council took advertising space to inform their poll tax payers: 'Because of its official opening, Midlothian House will be closed to all members of the public on Friday 22 November.'

HIGHLAND region advertised for a person to be i/c sewerage. As the advert stated, the successful applicant will be required to 'help bring out the best in Highland Region'.

OVERHEARD in a BBC canteen: 'Me pretentious? I used to be but I'm not *maintenant.*'

QUOTE from an Edinburgh legal chap envious of the $250,000 fee earned by an American lawyer for a trial: 'Och, it would take a Scottish solicitor a year to defraud a client of that amount of money.'

THE proliferation of forgeries of Bank of England £5 notes led to a degree of caution in retail premises. Thus this conversation between two check-out operatives in Safeway in Paisley in which the first (holding out a Bank of Scotland fiver to her colleague) asked for advice as to its authenticity. Second operative: 'Aye, that's OK. It's the wan wi' the wumman's heid we don't take.' The wumman she was referring to was none other than our own dear Queen.

DEPT of We Know What They Meant: The HMSO publication entitled *Sexual Harassment in the Workplace* advises: 'If a complaint is upheld you may need to separate the parties involved.' But hopefully not with a bucket of water.

JOHN Callan of Cowcaddens told of his time in the City Bakeries as part of a four-man nightshift squad making pancakes. A fifth man was added to the squad and the production of pancakes soared. This fifth chap was known as the extra man. 'Then one night the chap was off sick,' related

Mr Callan, 'and the wee gaffer (the gaffers apparently were always wee) was asked to explain why production was down.' He replied that the downturn pancakewise was because 'we were an extra man short'.

THE Diary does not normally endorse graffiti but we were prepared to make an exception in the case of a wee inscription in a lift at Mercantile Chambers in Bothwell Street, Glasgow. The offices of the Prince's Scottish Youth Business Trust are in the building. The Prince of Wales himself had visited and, by chance, the lifts had just been refurbished. The brown paint in one of the lifts had been scratched with the message 'HRH was ER.'

SIGN spotted attached to a defective turnstile at Cowcaddens Underground station in Glasgow: 'Broke – As in Not Working.'

DEPT of We Know What They Meant: A customer phoned a mail-order company and gave his address as 'Smith – seven oblique four Castle Wynd, Edinburgh'. He duly received a parcel addressed to 'Smith, 7 O'Bleak 4, Castle Wynd Edinburgh'.

A COMPANY called Adams Rental advertising in the American magazine *TV Facts*: 'Now renting Diamond Engagement rings and Wedding Bands – No Long Term Obligation.'

ADVERT for La Florida restaurant in

Tenerife: 'Due to popular demand, Sunday lunch is now served on Wednesday nights.'

OVERHEARD in the John Menzies shop at Glasgow Airport. An American lady is holding aloft a tartan-bedecked tin labelled 'Nippy Sweeties'. She asks the shop assistant: 'Hi! Can you tell me what these taste like?' To which the shop assistant helpfully replies: 'Ah'm no awfy sure, but ah think they taste something like Soor Plooms.'

BRITISH Home Stores, seeking for its store at the St Enoch Centre, Glasgow, an 'intimate-apparel manager' placed an advert stating that 'applicants must possess a hands-on approach'.

THE more all-seater stadiums proliferate, the less fun there is to be had on a sporting day out. Ask the Murrayfield debenture-holder who found the two seats behind him occupied by two women who gossiped all the way through a Scotland–Ireland match. Try as he might, he just couldn't concentrate on the game as one of the ladies told in some detail how her husband was having an affair with his secretary. All hope of paying attention to the game went out of the window when he heard the words: 'And honestly, I don't know what she sees in him. I haven't had an orgasm for six years.'

LORD James Douglas-Hamilton, the

Scottish Office roads minister famous for the common touch, asked as he was being driven along an Edinburgh street in the back of Scottish Office limo: 'Tell me. What exactly is a bus lane?'

OVERHEARD in a Maybole pizza parlour. 'Give me a big pizza with the trimmings.' 'Do you want it cut in four sections or eight?' asks the guy behind the counter. 'Better make it four. I don't think I could manage eight.'

DEPT of We Know What They Meant: The menu of an Italian restaurant in Cork bears the slogan: 'You will not get better.'

MYSORE, India, has a restaurant which boasts that its food 'will make more than your mouth water'.

THE *Co-operative News* carried a news story headed 'Funeral Directors Celebrate' which told us that one of their divisions is 'reporting strength in depth in the funerals' department'.

GREAT Pub Observations of Our Time: 'I wouldnae say the service is bad in this place but you could get a drink quicker in the Betty Ford clinic.'

'I wouldnae say it's a rough pub but at drinking-up they send in Kate Adie to collect the glasses.'

OVERHEARD while filing out after a bowling-club dance. First genteel lady: 'Did you see the eclipse of the moon the other night?' Second genteel lady: 'I didn't actually see it but I heard it on the radio.'

TALES of the Unexpected. An advertisement in the Borders weekly newspaper the *Southern Reporter* forlornly advised: 'Due to an error an evening of clairvoyance will NOT be held tonight in the Foresters Arms, Jedburgh.'

AN outbreak of humour at Fife Regional Council, where they were discussing statistics in the chief constable's annual report. Councillor Tam Dair remarked that he always looks at the bottom of the statistical tables first and added: 'Mind you, I am a Cowdenbeath supporter.'

AN extract from a letter sent by a Strathclyde education official to the headmaster of St Ambrose High School in Coatbridge, which had won the 1992 Curriculum Award: 'I would wish to pay my own personal tribute to yourself, your staff and, of course, your pupils for the magnificent work which must have went into the school's submission in order to achieve the award.'

SEE Glasgow? See culture? The Diary normally shuns toilet talk but was impressed by the following conversation in the gents at (where else) the Centre for Contemporary Arts in Sauchiehall Street after a show of avant-garde theatre.

Man at first urinal: 'Spirituality is still an important element in society . . .'

Man at second urinal: 'No, I doubt the relevance of spirituality in life today . . .'

Voice from second cubicle on left: 'Surely first of all you have to define spirituality . . .'

SLOGAN on the side of a van belonging to an Asian-owned building company in Bradford: 'You've Used the Cowboys, Now Try the Indians'.

STRATHCLYDE police informed the media that '8,000 tons of EC mince' had been stolen from a Salvation Army warehouse in Cambuslang before it could be distributed to local OAPs. While the collective journalistic mind was attempting to cope with the concept of how anyone could purloin such a large amount of mince, the polis were on to say it was in fact 8,000 tins of mince which had been nicked.

FOLK singer Hamish Imlach told in his autobiographical tome, *Cod Liver Oil and the Orange Juice* (£7.99 in a bookshop near you), that he had an allergy to leather – every time he wakes up in bed with his shoes on he has a terrible headache. We asked readers if they suffered similar afflictions. Eric V. Hudson of Bearsden recalled his days as a Round Tabler and a colleague who, as he donned his dinner jacket before departing for the soirée, was asked by his darling three-year-old daughter: 'Daddy, why do you wear that jacket? You know it always makes you sick.'

NAME GAME

CASTLE Douglas down in bonnie Galloway boasts a dental surgeon in King Street by the name of Aitken Grieve.

READER Paul Trevisan of Glasgow was intrigued by the morning-after connotations of a dish featuring on the menus of sundry Indian restaurants. It is called sali boti.

A FIRM of property developers were spotted in Cumnock, Ayrshire, by the name of Steele and Cosh.

THE organiser of a conference in Newfoundland on the subject of 'Training for Survival at and Rescue at Sea' was a Captain Drown.

AUTHORESS of an article entitled 'Going for a pint, girls?' in *The Dear Green Pint*, Camra's guide to Glasgow's real-ale joints, was one Ellen McSwiggan.

A NUMBER of British Airways passengers have been in touch to tell us of a little discovery they made while stuck far longer than planned on the Shuttle. They whiled away the extra hours reading *High Life*, the BA mag-azine, where they found the fascinating information that the airline's head of planning was a Mr Rod Muddle.

A DIARY reader soujourning in Malmesbury, Wiltshire, reported that a local coffee shop is owned by one Jill Eatwell. Then there was the chap in the Inland Revenue enforcement section in Edinburgh with the biting name, Mr I. Bark.

THE chap given the task of explaining to the shop assistants at Harrods that times were tough and there would have to be a wage freeze was a Mr Bollinger. Not 'Champagne Charlie' but plain Peter Bollinger.

HARLAND and Wolff of Belfast is building six ships specially designed to carry ore and coal around the difficult waters of the Cape of Good Hope. They are to be called Capesize-class ships – not a very safe-sounding name, especially when pronounced in a Kelvinside or Morningside accent.

A FAST-FOOD chain specialising in French fries (a chip shop to youse) in Saudi Arabia rejoices in the name Badkook and Sons.

140

THE British Wellness Council launched National Condom Week (slogan: Slip into Something Safe and Sexy) and took the sensible precaution of appointing as Condom Week press officer a lady called Emma Cox.

VACANCIES were advertised for store detectives by HMV, the high-street music chain. Aspiring crimestoppers were asked to apply to a Mary Cotmore.

The Engineer magazine reported that the flushing toilet, as invented by Thomas Crapper more than 100 years ago, is to be superseded by a new toilet, the Somerfield solid-state syphon. But, as *The Engineer* points out, it will not be the same: 'That's a load of Somer just doesn't have the right sort of ring to it, does it?'

FOR no particular reason at all, we would like to inform you that in the town of Wallington, Surrey, there is a street by the name of Senga Road.

THE manager of the British bobsleigh team for the 1992 Winter Olympic Games was one Colin Snowball.

IN Tonah Rata, Malaysia, there is a takeaway food store called the Chip Fatt Shop.

MANAGER of Kelvingrove Park, Glasgow, is a Mr Jim Chestnut.

WINNER of the Financial Director of the Year Award 1992 was a Mr Brian Fidler.

ONE of Washington's leading claims lawyers is Phyllis Outlaw.

SCOTTISH Enterprise sponsored a symposium on Sewage Sludge Disposal, The Commercial Opportunities, at which a lecture on the topic of Existing Scottish Disposal Arrangements was delivered by Dr Mike Heap of Lothian regional council.

A CHAP ordained to appear at Stranraer Sheriff Court on a charge alleging assault was one John Brawls.

BY deciding not to use her husband's name, Baroness Lynda Chalker has deprived the House of an interesting name. She is mairrit oan to one Clive

Landa. So she could have been Lady Lynda Landa.

HEAD of religious education at BBC Wales is one Mair Pope.

MOTHER India's Café, Glasgow's original low-cost restaurant offering traditional home-cooking from the subcontinent, occupies premises previously called The Bad Ass Club.

THE Howard Committee for Penal Reform has a member by the name of Francis Crook.

A LECTURE to the Geological Society of London titled 'Explosive Volcanic Eruptions' was given by Dr Steve Sparks of Cambridge University.

GERMAN tourists are famous the world over for their aggressive attitude. So it is perhaps not surprising that a London company offering package holidays to Germany should be called GTF Tours.

THE picket lines at strike-bound BBC headquarters in Glasgow were crossed by a gent by the name of Mr Pidgeon. Justified or not, he was henceforth referred to as Scabbie Doo.

THE leading firm of undertakers in Cape Town rejoices in the name Human and Pitt.

THE chap appointed as consultant to the project to recover the contents of the sunken whisky galore ship, SS *Politician*, was a Mr Davie Jones.

THE director of the Derbyshire Centre for Integrated Living is Mr Peter Pine-Coffin.

THE Scottish Prison Service launched a newspaper for its staff. It was called *The Informer*. This appears, to the Diary, an infelicitous choice with overtones of sneaks, grasses and stool pigeons. Much better, surely, would have been *News of the Screws*.

WHO could resist a make-over at the Hackett Beauty Centre, London?

THE Events Suppliers Association appointed a new chairman, a Mr Cliff Ball of the Humping Company.

HERO of the hour when fire broke out at the Myreton Motor Museum, Aberlady, was the curator who alerted the fire brigade and then contained the flames. He is a Mr Match.

A Mr J. Mycock holds the position of controller of small parts at Rolls-Royce, Derby.

THE vicar of the Church of St James in Devizes, Wiltshire, is the Rev. Tim Pape.

GUEST of honour at the annual dinner of the Institute of Company and Commercial Accountants in London was one Lord Eatwell.

THE author of the American edition of the *Illustrated Encyclopaedia of Sex* is Dr A. Willy.

ROSS Perot, that awfy nice wee billionaire who ran for the US presidency in 1992, had a campaign manager called Orson Swindle.

WE were intrigued to hear that Paisley has an eating establishment by the name of Café Borgia. As in: 'Hello, my name is Lucrezia. I'm your waitress for tonight.'

FULL-BACK at the Wasps rugby club in London is one Alan Buzza.

AN Edinburgh establishment goes by the name of the El Paso Driving School. We are less certain of the allure of the Edinburgh restaurant which boasts the name Pancho Villa's Dry Boak Gulch.

THE Diary reported the missed opportunity of Dumfries and Galloway police to have the street housing their new HQ named Annapolis Street, after the Doonhamers' twin toon in the United States. An appropriate alternative name for the new thoroughfare to the cop shop might have been Letsby Avenue.

THE catering manager at Cleland Hospital rejoices in the name I. Tipple.

THE executive chef of The Mandarin Oriental in Hong Kong is one Mr Munch.

EXECUTIVE producer of the BBC programme *A Secret World of Sex* was one Sam Organ.

DIRECTOR of customer satisfaction at Avis Europe is one Linda Lash.

THE threat that some of Scotland's famous regiments may be amalgamated with their English counterparts raised the vexed question of what these hybrid units might be called. The Duke of Wellington's Regiment might merge with the Royal Green Jackets to become the Royal Green

Royal Army Dental Corps appear, on the face of it, to have something in common. They could become the Dental Lancers. The Army Legal Corps will no doubt join up with the Parachute Regiment to form a corps of crack solicitors who can drop behind enemy lines and sue people. Crossing the geographical boundaries we could have the King's Own Scottish Kent Yeomanry.

It is surely only a matter of time before cutbacks force the Army to form alliances with outside agencies and even private enterprise. Thus the Boy Scouts and the Queen's Own Highlanders could form the Boys' Own Highlanders. The Guards Division could save money by amalgamating with Group 4 to form the Group 4 Security Guards regiment.

Wellingtons. The Royal Electrical and Mechanical Engineers could join forces with the Argyll and Sutherland Highlanders and be known as the Royal Electrical and Mechanical Highlanders. The Lancers and the

144

DELAWARE

On one of those many quiet days, when there was nothing with which to fill the Diary, we went to the pub and came back with the concept of Why Did Achiltibuie? It was based on a Scottification of the old Perry Como song *What Did Delaware?* So among other questions we asked, why did a kiltie boo ye? The answers came in thick and fast. Like:

I called him Kelty, Kelty cauld bum.
I don't know but I'll Wormit oot o' him.
He wisnae Uist tae me wearing Y-fronts on my Beattocks.
Because of the Moniaive squandered on troosers.
Because I passed some Foula Ayr and caused an Achnastank.
Because I put out my Tongue and said Iona new Glen Garry.
Because Islay on his Glen Garry.
Because I had my Bonnyton instead of my Glen Garry.
Because I Caldham a Brolass.
Because I Coll-ed him the Crook of Devon, after he'd Tain my Dollar, which really got on my Wick.
Because I stole his Galloway and

my sporran was Biggar.
Because his kilt was Stornoway.
Because real men wear Nethan under their Cults.
Because his manners were Kindallachan.

Why was Gorbals Cross?
Because he couldn't Mount Florida.

What attracted the Maidens?
Brodick.

What did Penicuik?
She cooked a Currie for her Five Sisters.

What made Achnasheen?
Some Spittal of Glenshee.

Why did Arthurlie?
To get a Ballygrant.

What achievement made Auchencrow?
Bowling the Maidens over.

Why did Auchenshuggle?
His underpants had come Luce.
Because he was frightened of Ardlui.

145

Forres Foula Rhum.
After taking a Drem he thought he
  saw Strathtummel.
Because he saw Dumbarton Rock.
He was in front of a Jura and he
  knew he'd Dunnet.
He had to sit in Kirk a' day.

What made Macmerry?
Kippen with Aberlady.
A Doll who would go Alloway.
He liked Salen and made a Kerrera
  it.
He Gott Foula Rhum.
He was Sluggan Rhum and Methil
  spirits and getting Slochd and
  fallin Doune. But he couldn't
  buy it on the Sleat.
Because Kittybrewster was a
  Fairlie easy Touch for a Loan.

What did Colonsay?
I must Staffa drink but I won't take

the car because drinking and driving is Eriskay business.

Kinross come out to play?
Aye, he'll be Doune the stair in a
  minute wi' his Barra.
Naw, he Canna. He's covered in
  Muck and his dad, Ed, is mad.
  And when Ed's mad, Edzell.

Who stole Hunter's Quay?
Tillicoultry Dunnett.
Suspicion points Toward Cove but
  nobody's Kirn.

How much is Polwarth?
Loads of Monzie.
Alva Dollar.

How did Glendaruel?
She sang Forres a grand old team
  to play for.
She always called the Shotts.
She beat the King-u-ssie.
She never let Colintraive her to
  drink or get under Erskine.
She ruled with a Methil fist.
I Dairsie with Ferness.
Inellan's favour.
With a Lochgelly.
Very well, as it 'Appins.
She gave no Quarter.
Like all Queensferry well.

In this same vein a reader informed us
of a splendid Scottish place name version of the royal coat of arms which
runs: Onich Soit Qui Mallaig Pense.
This translates as: You might think
you're in Mallaig but you're only in
Onich.

It was at this point that someone observed that Thurso many possibilities but does anyone Gigha damn?

Islay odds Williamwood, Girvan the chance, came the swift reply.

USEFUL

ONE of the Diary's favourite topics is Things You Never Knew You Wanted Until You Saw It In A Catalogue. Such as some of the unusual items on offer from The Engine Shed mail-order railway-model company. Especially arcane is their list of the wee people that can be purchased to populate the trackside of your average model-railway complex. The list includes your standard groups like 'waiting passengers', 'track maintenance gang', and 'arriving passengers'. Then, further down the list, do we not find 'wedding group, Protestant' and 'wedding group, Catholic'. What, we asked the man on the mail-order line at The Engine Shed, was the difference? Quite simple, he said.

In the Protestant wedding group the vicar is wearing black and in the Catholic one the vicar is wearing white. So far, so good if not an entirely accurate representation of the differences between Proddies and Tims. But our attention was then drawn to other items on the list like 'artist, sculptor, nude', 'nude bathers', and 'doctor, patient, revue girl'. We were particularly intrigued by this last category.

Explain, we asked the man at The Engine Shed. Quite simple, really. 'This group consists of a doctor with a female patient stripped to the waist, a striptease artist, a naked lady with a towel, another naked lady with her arm covering her bosom, and a lady in a leotard.' Yes, of course, just another day in the doctor's surgery. (Does the BMA disciplinary tribunal know about this chap?)

We didn't like to ask but we presume that the respective groups advertised as 'shepherd with dog and sheep' and 'boy scouts' are more mundane and of a different stamp from the doctor and his coterie of floozies. We should add, in defence of Britain's railway modellers, that the above items are manufactured in Germany. And they carry a warning that they are 'recommended for model builder and collectors as of 14 years of age.'

OTHER Essential Items:

The Swiss Lady Fertility Watch which 'uses the natural laws of the menstrual cycle to help parents plan for a baby boy or girl. Tests carried out in Germany, and supported by the German Research Foundation, show that Swiss Lady's timing has a 90 per cent success rate.'

This combination of Germanic efficiency and Swiss accuracy will 'help you keep a check on the right time for conception'. So how does it work? 'There's no need for complex calculations or complicated charts – you simply follow the easy instructions supplied.' We asked just how easy were these easy instructions. Actually, the watch comes with four A4 pages of instructions. The lady on the telephone confessed that she could not give us a simple, brief version. The watch is 'beautifully styled so it can be worn as an ordinary watch'. The watch face is black and green with the rather unsubtle logo of an apple with a bite out of it. So watch out. If you see a lady wearing such a watch, it is probably best not to ask her if she has the time. Another piece of totally useless, but interesting, information about the Swiss Lady

Fertility Watch is that it is waterproof to 100ft.

FROM the Pets Pleasure mail-order catalogue we present 'the new-style dog's waxed jacket with turn-back corduroy collar, suitable for either country or smart town wear'. It doesn't say if the doggie's waxed jaiket includes a poacher's poacket.

Also irresistible is the selection of kebab-shaped munchy treats on a biscuit skewer. Suitable, we presume, for smartly dressed dogs seeking a takeaway after a night out on the town.

BEANO, a product advertised in *Alive*, the Canadian Journal of Health and Nutrition, claims to be a 'revolutionary way to prevent gas'. It is a magic potion hailed as 'a new scientific and social breakthrough that helps to prevent wind from beans, broccoli, cabbage, whole-grain cereals and many other legumes and vegetables'. In fact, 'Beano lets you and your family enjoy today's healthful foods without most gas distress.'

Also from North America – 'Haemorr-ice, an insertable rod for cooling and shrinking haemorrhoids'.

ANTIKA Sherds: 'Solve the riddle of the sands. Dig up sherds from their simulated desert sand, match the pieces and restore them, just as an archaeologist would. The result is a beautiful collector's piece that you will treasure and your friends will admire. Antika sherds are authentic replicas from a bygone age, hand-made by native potters using skills passed down through the centuries. Each pot is then turned into sherds just as the originals were shattered in the mists of time.' The result is a cracked pot for any crackpot to put on their mantelpiece. An archaeological adventure. Or perhaps, at £24.95, a very expensive and silly 3D jigsaw.

LANGUAGE AND THAT

SUCH was the volume of purchases by a lady at a supermarket that, while she was struggling to arrange them into tidy mountains of comestibles at the checkout, a box of cornflakes landed at her feet. On picking it up, and not knowing from which end of the conveyor belt it had escaped, she asked the girl at the till: 'Was this through?' To which the girl replied, in hurt and offended tones: 'Naw, it jist fell!'

AS part of the new freedom enjoyed by Russians, the Avis Press has been allowed to publish the *International Dictionary of Obscenities – A Guide to Dirty Worlds and Indecent Expressions*. Here are some of the less obscene examples:

- *Bzd'et*: To fart silently.
- *Loshka gavna v bochki m'oda*: A fly in the ointment. This translates literally as 'a spoonful of shit in a barrel of honey'.
- *Davalka*: Nympho.
- *Bros' dumat' zhopay*: Quit thinking with your ass.
- *Kakat*: To poop.
- *Irdun*: A person who farts frequently.

OVERHEARD on a North Sea ferry: A Scottish granny is admonishing her half-German grandwean: 'Gretchen! If ye dinnae stoap that you'll get yer heid in your hauns to play wi'.'

A VALUABLE document, a compendium of correspondence sent over the years to various departments of the Western Isles Council, came into the Diary's hands. The following examples highlight the very serious problem of thinking in Gaelic and writing in English:

- I am writing on behalf of my sink, which is running away from the wall.
- The toilet seat is cracked – where do I stand?
- This is to let you know there is a smell coming from the man next door.
- I request permission to remove my drawers in the kitchen.
- Our lavatory seat is broken in half and is now in three pieces.
- Will you please send someone to mend our broken path. Yesterday my wife tripped and fell on it and she is now pregnant.

151

- Our kitchen floor is very damp, we have two children and would like a third, so will you please send someone to do something about it.
- This is to let you know that our lavatory seat is broken and we cannot get BBC2.
- The toilet is blocked and we cannot bath the children until it is cleared.
- The lavatory is blocked. This is caused by the boys next door throwing their balls on the roof.
- I want some repairs doing to my cooker as it has backfired and burnt my knob off.
- Would you please send a man to look at my water, it is a funny colour and not fit to drink.
- Would you please send a man to repair my spout, I am an old-age pensioner and I need it straight away.
- I awoke this morning and found my water boiling.

ALSO germane to the subject of thinking in Gaelic and writing in English is this story from farthest Stornoway. A lady living on the rugged outskirts of said town had an arrangement with her butcher to send her an order of meat on a weekly basis, as travelling all the way into Stornoway for a leg of lamb or two was a wee bit too much for her.

One week, however, she decided she didn't need any meat, as her husband was going to slaughter a sheep for the freezer. Her telegram to the butcher was brief: 'Send no meat. Donald is killing himself.'

STILL on the subject of the Gaelic and the English, a Highland chentleman known to the Diary was explaining to us monoglots how the daily tasks in his household are split between the two languages. When he's taking the weans for a nice walk in the park or some other treat, conversation is conducted in Gaelic. When he has the unhappy duty of scolding a child, it is done in English.

FILMS

AS more and more Gaelic programmes hogged prime viewing time on Scotland's TV stations, the Diary put forward the suggestion that the annual £10m budget of the Comataidh Telebhisein Gaidhlig might be better spent on a truly blockbuster movie. Various suggestions as to possible titles soon came flooding in:

Home Ochone: Lost in Uist
Jurassic Park Bar
Wee Free Men and a Baby
An American in Harris
The Rocky Morar Picture Show
The Great Tain Robbery
Kisimul Kate
For a Few Shielings More
Plaid Again Sam
Out of Affric
Seven Sheep for Seven Brothers
Ceilidh's Heroes
Calum X
Full Tweed Jacket
High Dunoon
Every Which Way But Lewis
Born Wee Free
Wee Free Amigos
Sabbath, Bloody Sabbath
Two Muileachs for Sister Sara
The Crinan Game

Nuns on the Rhum
Blade Rona
The Tain Commandments
Lorna Dounreay
The Scarba Pimpernel
Brora! Brora! Brora!
Vaternish Down
From Here to Ettrick Bay
Flash Invergordon
Peggy's Ewe Got Married
Shinty Shinty Bang Bang
Cyrano de Berneray
The Great Golspie
Sleeping Beauly
Conan the Barra Bairn
Apokeachips Now

Worthy of a world première on a rainy night in Oban were:

It's a Mod, Mod, Mod, Mod World
Children of a Lesser Mod
Obanator and the follow-up
Obanator Dhu
A Streetcar Named Kintyre
Plaid Runner
Desperately Seeking Objective One
Status
Crofter Kane
Rebel Without a Croft
Where Seagulls Dare
Single White Cheviot

Who Will Have Had Their Dinner?
Some devious entrants tried to curry favour with our sponsors (a famous whisky company) by suggesting such titles as *Glengoyne with the Wind* and *Glengoyne Glen Ross*.

Elvis Presley was an inspiration for such Scottish remakes as *Love Me Senga, Follow That Dram*, and *Viva Lasswade*. Not to mention *Loving Ewe*. *In Bed with Ma Donald* saw a more recent pop icon Gaelicised.

It became necessary to open a special category for incredibly contrived titles, such as *Fried Clootie Dumpling at the Kyleakin Hotel* and *Ah Pauchle the Nips Now*.

Non-Gaelic-speaking areas soon demanded their own movies, the Northern Isles inspiring:

Conan the Orcadian
Yell Freedom
Hoy Noon
The Unsters
No Orcadians for Miss Blandish
Hoy Anxiety

And *Fair Isle Attraction* – you know the movie where Glenn Close rips off Michael Douglas's cardigan in a steamy sex session.

Speakers of the Doric tongue made a strong case for £10m a year to make their own movies, including a remake of that wonderful musical *Three Quines in a Fountain* and these:

The Loon's A Balloon
Grampian the Wonder Horse

The Sword and the Scone
The Cuillin Fields
The Spey Who Came in from the Cold
The Bodach Snatchers
Invasion of the Bothy Thatchers
Ossians Eleven
When Barra Met Islay
Honey I Shrunk the Kilts
Padraig Post Always Rings Twice

The Murdo movies were very popular:

Murdo Most Foul
Murdo She Wrote
Murdo and His Amazing Technicolor Tweed Jacket
Murdo on the Orient

Edinburgh did not feature by name but was obviously the setting for *Guess*

FILMS

Laurencekirk of Arabia
Bothy Nichts Fever
It's a Maud, Maud, Maud, Maud
  World

Turra! Turra! Turra!
Fit Like Doc?

FRECOSSAIS

IT came as a pleasant surprise while doing our bit for European unity in the single market in Normandy to discover that one of the cheeses which was receiving laldy is actually named after the Glasgow dormitory town of Bishopbriggs. For the benefit of those without a smattering of French, we are, of course, referring to Pont L'Eveque. This happy coincidence, or perhaps it was the Calvados chasers, led us to ponder on French versions of other Scottish place names, for instance, the three large residential quartiers of Glasgow known as Chateau du Lait, Paques-Maison, and Tambour-Chapelle. More chic addresses in the Glasgow area would include: Colline-Tete, Taniere-des-Ours, and Moulin-Individu. Heading out into Lanarkshire we find such places as Colline-des-Cloches and Les-Deux-Sont-Bien.

The Gallic Gazetteer was soon full of readers' suggestions:

Janvier-Decembre (Callender)
Un-Peu-d'Amour-Physique
   (Bonkle)
Je-Possede-Un (Iona)
L'Argent-J'ai (Moniaive)
Chien-Colline (Muthill)
Odeur-Tu-Lai (Mingulay)
La Ville d'Imposteur
   (Maxwelltown)
Terre-Derriere (Hyndland)
Petit-Verre-de-Kelvinside (Drem)
Claque-Mon-Pain-Indien
   (Slamannan)
Deteste Jean (Lothian)
Pleure-Dans-Un-Vert (Gretna
   Green)
L'Etoile-Propre (Anstruther)
Sans-Vache (Kyleakin)
Parbleu-en-Agiter
   (Auchenshuggle)
Eglise-Vache-Fromage
   (Kirkcudbright)
Peau-de-Derriere (Erskine)
Abeille-Parlez (Beatock)
Il y a Tant (Thurso)
J'ai Courru (Arran)
Mere-Grosse (Moffat)
Quel-Ruisseau (Whitburn)
Fini-Pechant (Dunsinnan)
Eglise-Tout-Le-Jour (Kirkcaldy)
Dormant (Kippen)
Partant (Leven)
Regrettez (Rhu)
Occupe (Tain)
Ma-Jambe (Mallaig)
Allez-Camionette (Govan)
Cuisine-Indienne (Currie)

A stretch of the imagination is required for the likes of:

Un-Ours-Mourant (Aberdeen)
Un-Ours-Serieux (Aberdour)
C'est-Dechire-Loin (Stornoway)
Benediction-un-Foin-Camionette (Bunnahabhainn or Boon a Hay Van)

Eventually notre tete was nipping with having to do so much translation of:

Verre-Allez (Glasgow)
Matin-Cote (Morningside)
Manteaux-Salees (Saltcoats)
Tuez-L'Archeveque (Kilwinning)
Salle-de-L'Alouette (Larkhall)

Chateau-sans-Chien (Castle Douglas)
Bateau-Beau-Thé (Broughty Ferry)
Port-Maison-de-Rapide (Gatehouse of Fleet)
Nouvelle-Tonne-Ragout-Art (Newton Stewart)
La-Ville-de-Qui (Houston)
Tuez-Le-Petit-Jacques (Killiecrankie)
Camionette-Egaree (Strathaven)
Lancy-Le (Hurlet)
Ils-Sont-D'Accord (Thurso)
Port-des-Dents-des-Hommes (Port of Menteith)

Even the map of the Verre-Allez Metro (Glesca Subway) came in for translation with such stops as Credit-au-Pair (Partick), Palais de Lally (Buchanan Street-Concert Hall), and Stade Edouard-Ours (Ibrox).

Being awfy linguistic, the teachers from Kyle Academy knew that zizi is French for willy. Thus there is that nice wee toon on Arran called Beau-Zizi (Brodick). And you will have noticed how often the snow blocks the road between Pont de Zizi and Chat-en-Outil.

Meanwhile back to the list:

Tuez-Mon-Peigne (Kilmacolm)
Venez-Frappez (Cumnock)
Voleur-Ville (Crookston, Glasgow)
La Ville de L'Oreille (Lugton)
Jambon-Fourbe (Cunninghame)
Tuez-Le-Fils-de-Monsieur-Nesbitt (Kilbirnie)
Colline de L'Art Nouveau

157

(Newarthill)
En-Haut-Loi-Lande (Uplawmoor)
Muet-Fritures (Dumfries)
Huit (Echt)
Deux-Centimetres-en-Blanc
(Whiteinch. There are actually
2.53 centimetres in an inch but we
won't quibble.)

A follower of a well-known West
End of Glasgow football club, Le
Chardon (Thistle), spoke of his many
happy hours spent at Le Mont des
Sapins. On the subject of football,
numerous folk suggested Parc-Tete
as the obvious translation of
Parkhead. We felt it might be more
accurate in those difficult days to call
it A La Recherche de Temps Perdu.

We now know that Kelso comes
from the French Quel-Sot, meaning
'What an idiot!' Dundee is renamed
Jute-Alors and Aberdeen, in tribute to
the renowned generosity of the
denizens of Furryboots City, has been
renamed Les Miserables. L'Ile-De-
Quel-Klaxon is, of course, Isle of
Whithorn. Poseur-Colline is, as you
probably knew, the Camphill area of
Glasgow. Ville-Des-Amoureux you
will recognise as Winchburgh. But,
enough of the Gallic Gazetteering.
Fini. Or Je-Sortirai as Alloway is now
known.

THE use of this Gallic–Scottish, or
Frecossais as some came to call it, was
not just limited to place names. We
heard of an instance in Lanarkshire
when a bon viveur in an estaminet in
Mere-Bien one night ordered a round

in French. 'Cinq demis de cloches,
Jacques,' he cried. A young lady sitting near the bar asked her boyfriend
what had just been said. He replied
gravely: 'He said it's half-past five.'

A PARTY of Glasgow councillors
made the pilgrimage to see Rangers
playing Marseille in the European
Cup. On the return journey they were
shopping in the duty-free section at
Paris Charles de Gaulle airport. One
of the cooncillors decided that an
Easter egg would be a splendid present for the wife. He approached the
mademoiselle behind the counter
with the words: 'Any Easter eggs?'
Predictably, the young lady did not
understand. The cooncillor returned

to his chums for some advice on matters linguistic and duly returned to the jeune fille with the amended question: 'Any Easter oeufs?'

A similar conversation involving a Scottish customer in French shop: 'Oeufs,' he says. Assistant: 'Douze?' Customer: 'Naw. Hen's . . .'

LOBEY DOSSER

ONLY two years late, on Friday, 1 May 1992, the statue of Lobey Dosser on his trusty steed El Fideldo was unveiled in Woodlands Road, Glasgow. The idea of a memorial to cartoonist Bud Neill was launched by the *Herald* Diary as an event for Glasgow's Year of Culture in those heady early days of 1990.

The public reaction to the idea was immediate, positive, and overwhelming. The £10,000 budget was reached within two months amid a veritable spate of Neillian memories. It seemed that the euphoria would carry on to the ambitious planned unveiling date of Glasgow Fair Friday, 1990.

So what happened? After the euphoria, reality quickly set in. With a combination of a naïve journalist (that's me, folks) in charge and an artist (Calum MacKenzie, who came up with the original idea) who is very good at the concepts but not very hot on the detail, it was perhaps inevitable that the plan should go agley. Calum's budget of £10,000 was hopelessly inadequate. Oh, and there was another detail I hadn't actually thought to check before launching the project. Calum MacKenzie was a painter to trade and couldn't actually build a statue. But he knew a man who could.

Except, as it turned out, the man couldn't.

The Glasgow Fair of the Year of Culture came and went. I called in to check the progress on the maquette, the small-scale model of the statue. It consisted of a lump of expanded foam which someone had tried in a desultory fashion to turn into a model of Elfie carrying two riders, Lobey and Rank Bajin. It looked more like a camel, the kind with two humps. It had two matchsticks, one in each side of the head, apparently to hold on the ears.

I did not need independent art experts to tell me the project was going nowhere. Reading through the voluminous file of letters which the project had attracted, I found an ominous comment from Dr Sam McKinlay, editor of the *Evening Times* in the 1950s when Bud Neill's fame was at its height: 'I am glad the appeal has gone so well although I have a sneaking feeling that Bud should have been commemorated otherwise. I imagine it's going to be awfully difficult explaining the reason for the statue when it does appear.' Not as difficult,

I thought, as explaining why the statue wasn't going to appear at all.

Then there came a letter from a lady in her eighties who had sent £2 to help build the statue. She was afraid that with the delays she wouldn't live to see it built. It was a time of some despair.

Meanwhile, the Glasgow village rumour mill was working overtime. The whole thing was an elaborate practical joke, went one theory. Indeed, the cash had been misappropriated. The money was, in fact, nestling safely in the Clydesdale Bank under the watchful eye of Richard Cole-Hamilton, the bank's chief executive who had agreed to act as treasurer for the Lobey Dosser Statue Fund. My potential personal loss of credibility was bad enough; even worse was the ignominy of having involved respected public figures such as Mr Cole-Hamilton and Maria Fyfe MP and Lord Carmichael of Kelvingrove who had willingly joined the statue committee.

Then, in August 1990, help came from an unexpected source – Dundee. I met Bob Millar Smith, the ebullient director of Duncan of Jordanstone College of Art, at a performance in Glasgow by the Bolshoi Opera. He listened to my tale of woe and promised to help.

Within a matter of weeks, he was back in touch to say that he had two extremely talented sculptors in their final year at the college who might be able to help. The two students, Tony Morrow and Nick Gillon, were skilled modellers – artists who were interested in pursuing traditional statuary skills in an era when their contemporaries were assembling random objects and calling it a construction. Tony, a former fire-brigade mechanic from Glasgow who had turned to art, and Nick, his younger colleague from Edinburgh, were intrigued by the project and agreed to build the maquette. The clay model was completed in less than two weeks.

It was a brilliant piece of work by two young men who had known nothing of Bud Neill or Lobey Dosser (although some fellow students noted a similarity in looks between Tony and Lobey). They had brought a set of two-dimensional cartoon characters leaping out of the page without losing any of the Neillian magic.

The next stage was to build the life-size glass-fibre model from which the bronze statue would eventually (one day, we hoped) be cast. People in the sculpture business have told me that this part of the process should have been budgeted at anything between £5,000 and £10,000. Tony Morrow and Nick Gillon did it for the challenge.

Three months later the model was completed. Three months of late nights and working weekends, in addition to an already punishing schedule for their own final-year projects. Let no one be in any doubt. The Lobey Dosser statue is their work.

Tony and Nick made this project with their talent, their grit, and uncompromising, honest hard work.

BRIDIE McPHERSON

WE have to thank the National Museum of Science and Industry in London for some long overdue recognition of the Glasgow tram conductress. The museum had a drama programme in which they said: 'History comes to life with actors/interpreters inspiring children to learn about such colourful characters as Amy Johnson (Gypsy Moth); Thomas Crapper of flush-loo fame; Bridie McPherson, the Glasgow tram conductress; Michael Faraday, the father of electricity; and many more.'

There was, however, one question which sprang to mind: who the hell was Bridie McPherson? We wracked our brains and fully ten seconds later realised we had never heard of Bridie, the famous Glasgow tram conductress. Other famous Glasgow tram-lore brains were duly wracked but still there was no information on Bridie McPherson.

We asked the museum to cummoan gettaff and gie us an explanation. A very nice man called Guy Thomas, spokesman for the project, admitted that they had made up the Bridie character. But she was 'based on extensive research into the working lives of women on the trams'.

Bridie's character was 'ebullient, outgoing, extrovert and strong'. (You're telling us, pal, if she was typical of the tramcar breed.) The script which the museum drama project had concocted for Bridie included her having to cope with wee Glasgow drunk men and recalcitrant urchins.

While it was nice to see the Museum of Science and Industry in London keep Glasgow's tramcar history alive, us chaps at the Diary felt there should be some indigenous input. We asked our dear readers to come up with an authentic life story for Bridie.

Details soon emerged of the life and working times of Bridie McPherson, the Glasgow tram conductress.

WILLIAM Haddow of Pollokshields was quickly into the breach with a story about a group of Glasgow Yoonie divinity students who boarded a No. 3 tram and climbed to the upper saloon which was otherwise deserted. After Bridie had collected their fares they dared to interfere in her domain by turning round all the reversible seats and settling down to read their newspapers, thus giving pedestrians the impression that the caur was trundling backwards. Sensing something was amiss, Bridie investigated and chucked them all off with the ringing rejoinder: 'Wait until yiz come oot as ministers afore ye start pesterin' decent folk!'

MR M. JOYCE from Eaglesham remembered that Bridie was Amazonian in physique and temperament. She plied her trade on the old No. 7, commonly known as the Yella Caur, which went from Bellahouston to Riddrie. She could often be seen at either terminus changing the overhead trolley rope with her teeth, while counting the money in her cash bag.

BILL Waddell from Cumbernauld wondered if it was the one and same Bridie McPherson who attested in court that her driver, seeing an elderly pedestrian on the track, 'started tae stoap but couldnae go slow fast enough tae avoid a mis-hap'?

MRS D. BROWN from Helensburgh remembered Bridie McPherson when she took her 'Ha'penny Special' tram ride from Hillhead High School to the Hughenden playing fields on Great Western Road on games afternoon. As the tram slithered to a halt at the stop, Bridie would hang off the platform, hand extended to stop the rush and shout: 'Staun back! Staun back! It's the weans frae the potted heid school gaun' tae play games again!'

THE titan terror of the trams was well remembered by Mrs Alice Forsyth of Inverkeithing: 'Bridie stood five feet ten in her diamond-mesh stockinged soles. Her bosom was of such proportions that Black's of Greenock used one of her brassieres as the prototype for their igloo tents and she augmented her niggardly wage from the Corporation Transport department through a number of sponsorship deals with the manufacturers of peroxide, Polyfilla, and kirby grips, which last she used in vast numbers to secure her clippie's bonnet, worn folded in half and over the "French roll" below the bouffant hairstyle which added four inches to her natural height.' Mrs Forsyth's favourite memory of Bridie dates back to a wet winter night when she was travelling home to Parkhead. An elderly man, cold and wet and drunk, boarded the tram in the Gallowgate. Displeased at his inebriated presence, Bridie towered over him while he tried to find money to enable him to buy a ticket. Eventually he found a threepenny bit and asked the impatient Bridie, 'How faur kin ah go fur thruppence, hen?' Bridie heaved her bosom and tempered justice with compassion in her rejoinder, 'You may kiss the tips of my fingers and then get aff.'

DOUGLAS Brown from Stranraer recalled an incident when Bridie was going up the stairs wearing a rather tight short skirt which had ridden up a little. A downstairs passenger called out in the face of Bridie's fleshy rear, 'My, the full moon's out tonight.'

'Aye,' retorted Bridie, 'and there'll be a wee man in it tonight.'

THE unflappability of the Glasgow clippie was further well illustrated by Mr T. Hughes of Bellshill, who told of the Saturday-night drunk who boarded the tram at Glasgow Cross and asked Bridie for a fourpenny one to Springburn. 'It's a tuppenny wan fur you,' said the conductress. 'I said a fourpenny one,' he repeated. 'And I said a tuppenny,' insisted Bridie, 'to Castle Street and the Royal Infirmary. There's an axe stickin' oot the back o' yer heid.'

ELLEN Japp of High Blantyre told how Bridie coped with fare-dodgers: 'She noticed that one man sat every morning and stared out of the window, never offering his fare.' This despite Bridie using her considerable lung power in requesting that passengers tender their cash. Finally it all became too much for Bridie. She stepped off the tram at the next stop, walked round the outside until she reached the window where the man was sitting, held out her hand and mouthed the words: 'Ferrs, please!'

BRIDIE also did a stint on the Glasgow buses, where one of her drivers was a West Indian. An old lady stopped the bus to ask if its route took it along Main Street, Bridgeton. Bridie answered in the affirmative. To her great scunnerment, the old lady proceeded to walk to the front of the bus where she asked the driver the same question. He confirmed that the bus did indeed go along Main Street. The old lady climbed aboard to be greeted by these words from Bridie: 'Is that you happy, noo, ye've goat it in black an' white.'

JIM MacDonald of Drymen related how Bridie was once taken to task for wearing an excess of make-up. The actual words, from a troublesome female passenger, were: 'You've enough clairt oan yir face to make pancakes.' 'Aye, missus, an' you've enough fat oan yir erse tae fry them in,' she replied

F. CRAIG from Crow Road, Glasgow, was there on an occasion when Bridie was trying to eject a drunk from the platform of her tram. 'Get aff,' she said. 'Aff. O-F-F. Aff.'

DOUGLAS Gilchrist of Beauly told how his father-in-law was there the day Bridie took pity on a poor man who was being harassed by unthinking fellow passengers. The man was at the front of a queue waiting to alight from the tram. He was of a nervous disposition, the step was on the high side, and he was waiting for the tram to come to a complete halt before stepping off. The chap had what was called in those days a 'humphy back'. Seeing his predicament and irritated by the abuse he was receiving, Bridie leapt to his defence with a loud bellow: 'Gie the boy a chance. It's no' a parachute he's got in there!'

BRIDIE may have gone to the great caur depot in the sky but her spirit lives in Glasgow transportation circles. In fact, she appears to be working as a station announcer on the Glasgow Underground, or Subway as we prefer to call it. The scene is Hillhead station. Bridie announces that the Inner Circle is out of service and would passengers please use the Outer Circle. (Readers from furth of the city should contact their nearest Glaswegian for an explanation of that last bit.) The passengers dutifully move to the bit of the platform that serves the Outer Circle. Except for one chap who is still hovering at the Inner Circle side. Bridie comes back on the blower: 'Would passengers please note that the Inner Circle is out of services. Please use the Outer Circle . . . Aye, ah mean you!' Embarrassed passenger shuffles over to join the rest, many of them unable to conceal large grins.

MERCANTILE MENDICANTS

PLOYS used by street beggars become increasingly ingenious:

A BEGGAR in Central Station, Glasgow, cashed in on the Thatcherite principles of self-employment by asking: 'Gies a pound. I want tae start my ain business!'

THEN there was the ruddy-faced, bleary-eyed gentleman who demanded of a passer-by in a Paisley street: 'Hey pal, gonnae gies 42p so's ah can buy a *Herald* tae look for a job?' Or the more direct approach of a chap in Sauchiehall Street: 'Ur any o' youse bastards gonny gie me a f****** ten pence?'

A DENIZEN of Dennistoun was making his way home from a public house having purchased a fish supper. On Duke Street, he was accosted by a footpad with the words: 'Gies that fish supper or I'll batter your face.' He found it an offer he couldn't refuse.

A YOUNG couple walking along Kilwinning main street were approached by a young man carrying an empty petrol can. He explained that his car had run out of petrol, which was parked just up the road, and could they lend him £1 towards a gallon? The man was very grateful and insisted on having a name and address to send the money on to. Walking up the street where the car was supposed to be parked, Mr Dalziel and his fiancée were somewhat taken aback to find no vehicle.

AN Irishman stopped a man in Hope Street, Glasgow. He claimed he was delivering horses to Hamilton Racecourse but had somehow got lost and could he please direct him to the motorway. The passer-by obliged and in return the Irishman advised him to put his life savings on a horse running the next day at Kempton Park. In return for the priceless information he was asked to give the Irishman a silver coin for 'stable luck', and fished out his change. The Irishman quickly picked out two fifty-pence coins, touched his forelock, said the statutory 'Good luck to ye, surr,' and was gone. Needless to say there was no such gee-gee running at Kempton the next day.

A CHAP, reeking of alcohol, stopped a shopper in Buchanan Street in

169

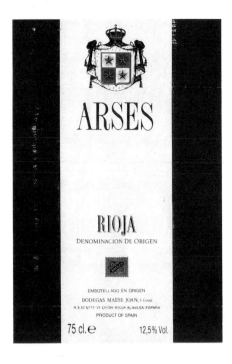

Cambuslang. One day in an area of the town noted for its Protestant tendencies, the street singer was giving a rollicking rendition of *Derry's Walls* and being showered with coppers by an appreciative audience. The next day, the same singer had a different song. In a back court of a part of Cambuslang occupied by people of another persuasion, he was delivering, hands clasped, as sweet a version of *Hail, Queen of Heaven* as you might have heard from Canon Sydney MacEwan himself.

ANOTHER begging victim was visiting a picture house in Portsmouth, when a chap offered to look after his car. A fee was agreed. As he entered the flicks, the beggar approached again and asked if he could have his fee upfront 'as I'll be going home in a few minutes'.

'COULD you spare 50p for a drink?' asked a mendicant in the West End of Glasgow. As people walked on, unimpressed, he changed his ploy too: 'American Express, Access, Visa . . .'

ONE Glasgow panhandler's dedication to business overcame his common sense. He was taken into police custody on another matter, and as he was put through the admission process at Barlinnie, the officers noticed a particularly obnoxious aroma emanating from the plaster cast on his leg. Questioned, the chap revealed that the stookie had been on for nearly a year and should have been

Glasgow with the curt message: 'Gies tempence [there is no N in tenpence, as you know] for a cuppa tea.' The shopper did so and jocularly added that the coin would no doubt go towards more drink. 'Listen, pal. What I do with my money is my business,' the mendicant replied. Along the same lines is the story of the shnorrer, a Yiddish beggar to you, who knocked upon a door to be told by the kindly but poor lady of the house: 'I'm sorry I don't have anything to give you today, but come back tomorrow.' 'Sorry, lady, I don't give credit,' he replied.

A READER recalled a back-street singer from his childhood days in removed some 10 months previously. Why had he not gone back to the hospital? 'It was a great help for the begging,' he revealed. Was he not concerned about the hygiene aspect? 'Well, I did give it two coats of emulsion when it got dirty,' he said.

BUT the prize for ingenuity goes to the Glasgow beggar who would accost clients with the words: 'Haw, chief, for a silly two boab I'll gie ye a bit of information that could save your life!' After the transfer of cash was completed, the mendicant enlightened donors with the words: 'Never take a lift hame in a car frae Edward Kennedy.'

DEEPLY PHILOSOPHICAL QUESTIONS

Why do aircraft toilets have frosted windows?

Did Paul ever get a reply from the Ephesians?

How many more witnesses do they need before Jehovah's trial starts?

How did the man who invented the bicycle know it was the bicycle?

Did the guy who lost the last chord have it insured?

If a brick lands on your head can you claim a lump sum?

Why, if John Smith wants to pursue a new moral politics and create an open society, does he keep avoiding the subject of Monklands District Council?

Allan Miller of Bishopton felt obliged to respond to our query as to whether anyone had ever seen a parson with a nose like a chicken's arse.

'The answer remains no,' says Mr Miller, 'but they must surely have hit the crossbar when they cast Karl Malden as the priest in *On the Waterfront*.'

Whatever happened to the first nine *Malcolm* movies?

Why is there no other word for synonym?

Why is there only one word for thesaurus?

Why is the alphabet in that order?

Why can't you buy inessential oils?

Why do people wear bum-bags at the front?

Why does sour cream have a sell-by date?

What was the greatest thing before sliced bread?

Where do the sick people of Lourdes go?

Why is abbreviation such a long word?

Why are water biscuits so dry?

Why, if Glasgow is such a great place, are there travel agents on every corner?

Why does the phrase 'Look, pal' in Glaswegian have nothing to do with friendship?

Why do people in Dumfries and Galloway region refer to Langholm as the Malvinas?

If a single bed is 3ft wide, how come a double bed is only 4ft 6in?

How do they always get fish the right size to fit the batter?

Why don8t typewriters have separate keys for apostrophes?

Who taught Kirkpatrick McMillan to ride a bike?

Whose bicycle pump did Dunlop borrow to blow up the first pneumatic tyre?

Why do badgers have such rough arses? And who discovered the fact?

What does acronym stand for?

What happened to First and Second Lanark?

Why do people only go to a health centre when they're ill?

How do you grow seedless grapes?

Where do *Scotsport* get the crowd noises for the first-division matches they feature on a Sunday, especially if the game is at Love Street?

Why can't we shuffle the letters in anagram to make any other words?

Why don't the United Nations declare Scotland a No Midge zone?

Why isn't a 4×4 vehicle simply known as a 16 vehicle?

Why do referees always use Partick Thistle colours when cautioning or sending off players?

What if nothing happens at the end of the day?

What will happen to the football pools if managers can't get a result?

Should a blind man pay for stairheid lighting?

If bankers can count, why do their counters have six windows but only two tellers?

Why is it that people who like a refreshment are always falling down?

Why do alarms go off instead of on?

Is acne an occupational hazard for football strikers, as in 'Duncan Ferguson picked his spot before tucking the ball away'?

Is the use of French phrases passé?

How did they measure hailstones before golf balls were invented?

Why is Jim Farry?

Did Rabbie Burns ever attend a James Currie Supper?

Has anyone ever actually eaten a Kellogg's pop tart for breakfast?

Why do seagulls fly upside down over Saltcoats?

Please note, we don't actually expect answers to our deeply philosophical questions.